Some Persons Un

E. W. Hornung

Alpha Editions

This edition published in 2023

ISBN : 9789357968959

Design and Setting By
Alpha Editions
www.alphaedis.com
Email - info@alphaedis.com

Contents

KENYON'S INNINGS

I

Kenyon had been more unmanageable than usual. Unsettled and excitable from the moment he awoke and remembered who was coming in the evening, he had remained in an unsafe state all day. That evening found him with unbroken bones was a miracle to Ethel his sister, and to his great friend John, the under-gardener. Poor Ethel was in charge; and sole charge of Kenyon, who was eleven, was no light matter for a girl with her hair still down. Her brother was a handful at most times; to-day he would have filled some pairs of stronger hands than Ethel's. They had begun the morning together, with snob-cricket, as the small boy called it; but Kenyon had been rather rude over it, and Ethel had retired. She soon regretted this step; it had made him reckless; he had spent the most dangerous day. Kenyon delighted in danger. He had a mania for walking round the entire premises on the garden wall, which was high enough to kill him if he fell, and for clambering over the greenhouses, which offered a still more fascinating risk. Not only had he done both this morning, he had gone so far as to straddle a gable of the house itself, shrieking good-tempered insults at Ethel, who appealed to him with tears and entreaties from the lawn below. Ethel had been quite disabled from sitting at meat with him; and in the afternoon he had bothered the gardeners, in the potting-shed, to such an extent that his friend John had subsequently refused to bowl to him. In John's words Master Kenyon had been a public nuisance all day—though a lovable one—at his very worst he was that. He had lovable looks, for one thing. It was not the only thing. The boy had run wild since his young mother's death. There were reasons why he should not go to school at present. There were reasons why he should spend the long summer days in the sunshine, and open only the books he cared about, despite the oddity of his taste in books. He had dark, laughing eyes, and a face of astonishing brightness and health: astonishing because (as he said) his legs and arms were as thin as pipe-stems, and certainly looked as brittle. Kenyon was indeed a delicate boy. He was small and delicate and weak in everything but spirit. "He has the spirit," said John, his friend, "of the deuce and all!"

Ethel forgave easily, perhaps too easily, but then she was Kenyon's devoted slave, who cried about him half the night, and lived for him, and longed to die for him. Kenyon had toned himself down by tea-time, and when he sought her then as though nothing had happened, she was only too thankful to catch his spirit. Had she reminded him of his behaviour on the roof and elsewhere, he would have been very sorry and affectionate; but it was not her way to make him sorry, it was her way to show an interest in all he had to say, and at tea-time Kenyon was still full of the thing that had excited and unsettled him in the morning. Only now he was beginning to feel in awe, and the schoolroom tea had never been a seemlier ceremony.

These children seldom sat at table with their father, and very, very seldom listened for the wheels of his brougham as they were listening to-night. In the boy's mind the sound was associated with guilty apprehensions and a cessation of all festivities. But to-night Mr. Harwood was to bring back with him one of Kenyon's own heroes, one of the heroes of his favourite book, which was not a storybook. It has been said that Kenyon's literary taste was peculiar; his favourite book was *Lillywhite's Cricketers' Guide*; the name of the great young man who was coming this evening had figured prominently in recent volumes of *Lillywhite*, and Kenyon knew every score he had ever made.

"Do you think he'll talk to us?" was one of the thousand questions which Ethel had to answer. "I'd give my nut to talk to him! Fancy having C. J. Forrester to stay here! I've a sort of idea the governor asked him partly to please me, though he says he's a sort of relation. I only wish we'd known it before. Anyhow, it's the jolliest thing the governor ever did in his life, and a wonder he did it, seeing he only laughs at cricket. I wish he'd been a cricketer himself, then he'd kick up less row about the glass; thank goodness I haven't broken any to-day! I say, I wish C. J. Forrester'd made more runs yesterday; he's certain to have the hump."

Kenyon had not picked up all his pretty expressions in the potting-shed; he was intimate with a boy who went to a public school.

"How many did he make?" Ethel asked.

"Duck and seven. He must be sick!"

"I shouldn't be surprised if he thinks far less about it than you do, Ken. It's only a game; I don't suppose he'll mind so very much."

"Oh, no, not at all; it's only about the swaggerest county match of the season," scathed Kenyon, "and they only went and let Notts lick! Besides, the *Sportsman* says he was out to a miserable stroke second innings. Where did I see the *Sportsman*? Oh, John and I are getting it from the town every day; we're going halves; it comes to John, though, so you needn't say anything. What *are* you grinning at, Ethel? Ah, you're not up in real cricket. You only understand snob."

Kenyon was more experienced. The public school boy hard by had given him an innings or two at his net, where Kenyon had picked up more than the rudiments of the game and a passion for *Lillywhite*. He had learnt there his pretty expressions, which were anything but popular at home. Mr. Harwood was a man of limited patience, with a still more limited knowledge of boys. He frightened Kenyon, and the boy was at his worst with him. A very sensitive man, of uncertain temper, he could not get on with his children, though Ethel was his right hand already. It was a secret trouble, an unacknowledged grief, to hard lonely Mr. Harwood. But it was his own fault; he knew that; he knew all about it. He knew too much of himself, and not enough of his children.

You could not blame Kenyon—Mr. Harwood would have been the last to do so—yet it was dreadful to see him so impatient for his father's return, for perhaps the first time in his life, and now only for the sake of the stranger he was bringing with him; to see him peering through the blind at this stranger, without so much as glancing at his father or realising that he was there; to hear him talking volubly in the drawing-room after dinner (when the children came down) to a very young man whom he had never seen before; and to remember how little he ever had to say to his own father. Ethel felt it—all—and was particularly attentive to her father this evening. That peculiar man may also have felt it, and the root of Ethel's attentions into the bargain; for he was very snubbing to her. He never showed much feeling. Yet it *was* to please Kenyon that Mr. Harwood had pressed Forrester to look him up, and not by any means (though this had been his way of putting it to his young kinsman, whom he scarcely knew) to cheer his own loneliness.

The cricketer was a sunburnt giant, disappointingly free from personal lustre, and chiefly remarkable for his hands. He had an enormous hand, and when it closed like jaws over Kenyon's little one, this suffering student could well understand his *Lillywhite* characterising C. J. Forrester as "a grand field, especially in the country." They talked cricket together from the first moment, and until Kenyon said good-night. Upstairs he told Ethel that so far they had got no further than the late match against Notts; that Forrester had described it "as if he'd only *seen* the thing;" and that she was quite right, and C. J. was far less cut up at the result than he was. It was Kenyon's county which had been trounced by Nottinghamshire, and he went so far as to affirm that C. J. Forrester's disappointing form had directly contributed to the disaster, and that he deserved to lose his place in the team. This, however, was but a drop of bravado in the first flood of enthusiasm for C. J.

Mr. Harwood watched and heard the frank, free, immediate intercourse between Kenyon and the visitor. He had never known Kenyon so bright and animated—so nearly handsome. The boy was at his best, and his best was a revelation to Mr. Harwood, who had never in his life had a real conversation with Kenyon such as Forrester was having now. He had talked *to* Kenyon, that was all. As he sat grimly listening, with Ethel snubbed to silence, he may have felt a jealous longing to be his small son's friend, not merely his father; to interest him, as this complete stranger was doing, and he himself honestly interested; to love openly, and be openly loved. The man was self-conscious enough to feel all this, and to smile as he rose to look at the clock, and saw in the mirror behind it no trace of such feeling in his own thin-lipped, whiskered face. At nine the children said good-night, of their own accord, knowing better than to stay a minute over their time. Mr. Harwood kissed them as coldly and lightly as usual; but surprised them with a pleasantry before they reached the door.

"Wait, Kenyon. Forrester, ask him your average. He'll tell you to a decimal. He knows what he calls his *Lillywhite* by heart."

Kenyon looked extremely eager, though Mr. Harwood's tone struck Forrester as a little sarcastic.

"You've been getting it up!" the cricketer said knowingly to Kenyon.

"I haven't," declared Kenyon, bubbling over with excitement.

"You needn't ask him your own," Ethel added, quite entering into it. "He knows them all."

"Oh, we'll have mine," said Forrester, who felt slightly ridiculous but much amused. "What was it for the 'Varsity—my first year?"

Kenyon had to think. That was three years ago, before he had known much about cricket; but he had read up that year's *Lillywhite*—he read as many old *Lillywhites* as he could borrow—and he answered in a few moments:

"Nineteen point seven."

"You *have* been getting it up!" cried Forrester.

Kenyon was beaming. "No, I haven't—honestly I haven't! Ask Ethel!"

"Oh, it's genuine enough," said Mr. Harwood; "it's his accomplishment— one to be proud of, isn't it? That'll do, Kenyon; good-night, both of you."

The door closed.

"*He's* one to be proud of," said Forrester pointedly, a vague indignation rising within him. "A delightful little chap, I call him! And he *was* right to a decimal. I never heard of such a fellow!"

"He's cricket mad," said Mr. Harwood. "I'm glad you like him."

"I like him immensely. I like his enthusiasm. I never saw so small a boy so keen. Does he play?"

"Not properly; he's not fit to; he's rather delicate. No, it's mostly theory with Kenyon; and I'm very much afraid he'll bore you. You mustn't let him. Indeed I fear you'll have a slow time all round; but, as I told you, there's a horse to ride whenever you want him."

"Does the boy ride?"

"He's not allowed to. Then we have a very respectable club in the town, where I can tuck you up and make you comfortable any time you like to come down. Only don't, for your own sake, encourage Kenyon to be a nuisance; he doesn't require very much encouragement."

"My dear sir, we're too keen cricketers to bore each other; we're going to be tremendous friends. You don't mean to say he bores *you*? Ah, with the scores, perhaps; but you must be awfully proud of having such a jolly little beggar; I know *I* should be! I'd make a cricketer of him. If he's as keen as this now, in a few years' time———"

"You smoke, Forrester? We'll go into the other room."

Mr. Harwood had turned away and was putting out the lights.

II

Long before breakfast next morning—while the lawns were yet frosted with dew and lustrous in the level sunlight—Kenyon Harwood and C. J. Forrester, the well-known cricketer, met and fraternised. Kenyon and John had always spoken of Forrester as "C. J."; and when Kenyon let this out, it was arranged, chiefly by C. J. himself, who was amused and pleased, that Kenyon should never call him anything else. Mr. Harwood, at breakfast, rather disapproved of the arrangement, but it was hardly a matter for the paternal ukase. Meanwhile Kenyon had personally conducted C. J. round the place, and had most impressively introduced him (in the potting-shed) to John, who looked so proud and so delighted as to put a head even on Kenyon's delight and pride. C. J. was charmed with John; but he was less enthusiastic about a bricked quadrangle, in front of the gardener's and coachman's cottages, with wickets painted on a buttress, where Kenyon was constantly indulging in small cricket—notably in the dinner-hour of John, who bolted his food to come out and bowl to him. The skilled opinion of C. J. was not in favour of "snob," as played by Kenyon with a racket and a soft ball.

"He says a racket is bad for you," Ethel understood from Kenyon (to whom it was a very serious matter); "makes you play with a crooked bat, and teaches you to spoon. So there's an end to snob! But what do you think? He's going to take me into the town to choose a decent bat; and we're going in for regular practice on the far lawn—John and all—if the governor lets us. C. J.'s going to coach me. Think of being coached by C. J. Forrester!"

"Father is sure to let you," said Ethel; and certainly Mr. Harwood did not say no; but his consent was coldly given, and one thing he stipulated almost sternly.

"I won't have Kenyon run. I shall put a stop to it if he does. It might kill him."

"Ah, he has told me about that." Forrester added, simply, "I am so sorry!"

Kenyon, in fact, in explaining the system of scoring at snob—a most ingenious system—had said:

"You see, I mayn't run my runs. I know the boundaries don't make half such a good game, but I can't help it. What's wrong? I'm sure *I* can't tell you. I've been to heaps of doctors, but they never say much to me; they just mess about and then send you back to the room where you look at the papers. Mother used to take me to London on purpose, and the governor's done so twice. It's my hip, or some rot. It's a jolly bore, for it feels all right, and I'm positive I *could* run, and ride, and go to school. Blow the doctors!"

"But obey them," C. J. had said, seriously; "you should go in for obeying orders, Kenyon."

They got the bat. It was used a great deal during those few days, the too few days of C. J.'s visit; and was permitted to repose in C. J.'s cricket-bag, cheek by jowl with bruised veterans that had served with honour at Lord's and at the Oval. Kenyon was very mindful of those services, and handled the big bats even more reverently than he shook his hero's hand. They lent themselves to this sort of thing more readily than C. J. did. Small doubt that Kenyon—at all events at first—would have had his hero a trifle more heroic than the Almighty had made him. There was nothing intrinsically venerable in his personality, as there might have been. He was infinitely more friendly than Kenyon had dreamt of finding him; he was altogether nicer; but he did lack the vague inexpressible distinction with which the boy's imagination invested the heroes of *Lillywhite's Guide*.

That summer was the loveliest of its decade, and Kenyon made the most of it. He had never before seemed so strong, and well, and promising. For the first time in his life his really miserable little body seemed equal—at moments—to his mighty spirit; and the days of C. J. were the brightest and happiest he had ever known. In that jolly, manly companionship the unrealised want of an intensely masculine young soul was insensibly filled. Hard, perhaps, to fill it so completely for so short a time: the cricketer's departure was so soon at hand! As it was he had put it off some days, because he liked Kenyon with an extraordinary liking. But he was wanted at the Oval on the last Thursday in July; his play with Kenyon and John (though John was a rough natural bowler) could by no stretch of imagination be regarded as practice for an important county match; he decided to tear himself away on the Tuesday morning.

He had been with them only a week, but the Harwoods had bitten deep into his life, a life not wholly consecrated to cricket. Forrester had definite aspirations, and some very noble intentions; and he happened to possess the character to give this spiritual baggage some value, in his case. Also he had a kind heart, which Kenyon had completely won. He liked Ethel; but one could not merely like Kenyon, with his frail little frame and his splendid spirit. Ethel, however, was very sweet; her eyes were like Kenyon's in everything but their sadness, as deep and lustrous, but so often sad. Her love for Kenyon was the most pathetic thing but one that Forrester had ever seen. The more touching spectacle was that of the father of Ethel and Kenyon, who seemed to have very little love for his children, and to conceal what he had. He was nice enough to Forrester, who found him a different being at the club, affable, good-natured, amusing in his sardonic way. He talked a little to Forrester about the children, a very little, but enough to make Forrester sincerely sorry for him. He was sorrier for Mr. Harwood than for Ethel or for Kenyon himself. He pitied him profoundly on Kenyon's account, but less because the boy might never live to grow up, than because, as Forrester read father and son, there would never be much love to lose between them. As for Kenyon, there was a chance for him yet: even the family doctor declared that he had never been so well as he was now. His vitality—his amazing vitality—seemed finally to upset a certain pessimistic calculation. His trouble might never become a greater trouble than it had been already; and this summer it had been no trouble at all, his very limp was no longer noticeable. He might yet go to school; and Forrester himself was going to start a small boys' school the following summer, in partnership with an older man, in one of the healthiest spots in the island. St. Crispin's had been spoken of for Kenyon. Kenyon himself spoke of little else during Forrester's last day or two. To go to school at St. Crispin's was now the dream of his life.

"I am sorry we told him about it," Mr. Harwood said, gloomily. "He may never be able to go there; he may never again be so well as he is now; all the summer it has seemed too good to last!"

Forrester, for his part, thought it good for the boy to have things to look forward to, thought that, if he could go, the change of life and climate might prove the saving and making of him. Beyond this, he honestly hoped for the best (whereas Mr. Harwood seemed to look for the worst), and expressed his hope—often a really strong one—with all possible emphasis.

He carries with him still some intensely vivid impressions of this visit, but especially of the last day or two, when the weather was hotter than ever—despite one splendid shower—and Kenyon if anything more alert, active and keen. He remembers, for example, how Ethel and Kenyon and he tore to an outlying greenhouse for shelter from that shower, or rather how he carried Kenyon. In the greenhouse, accompanied by a tremendous rattle of rain on the sloping glass, Kenyon sang them "Willow the King," the Harrow cricket song, which Tommy Barnard, the boy with the cricket-net, had taught Kenyon among less pretty things. Clear through the years Forrester can hear Kenyon's jolly treble, and Ethel's shy notes, and his own most brazen bass in the chorus; he even recollects the verse in which the singer broke down through too strong a sense of its humour:—

"Who is this?" King Willow he swore,
"Hops like that to a gentleman's door?
Who's afraid of a Duke like him?
Fiddlededee!" says the monarch slim.
"What do you say, my courtiers three?"
And the courtiers all said "Fiddlededee!"

But his last evening, the Monday evening, C. J. Forrester remembers best. They had an immense match—double-wicket. The head gardener, the coachman, John (captain) and the butler made one side; Forrester, Kenyon, Ethel (Kenyon insisted) and T. Barnard (home early, *æger*) were the other. "It's Gentlemen and Players," John said with a gaping grin; and the Players won, in spite of C. J., who, at the last, did all he knew, for Kenyon's sake.

It was a gorgeous evening. The sun set slowly on a gaudy scene; the wealth of colour was almost tropical. The red light glared between the trees, their crests swayed gently against the palest, purest amber. Mr. Harwood looked on rather kindly with his cigar; and the shadow of his son, in for the second time, lay along the pitch like a single plank. Ethel was running for him, and it was really exciting, for there were runs to get; it was the last wicket; and Kenyon, to C. J.'s secret sorrow, and in spite of C. J.'s distinguished coaching, was not a practical cricketer. Yet he was doing really very well this evening. They did not bowl too easily to him, he would not have stood that; they bowled very nearly their best; but Kenyon's bat managed somehow to get in the way, and once he got hold of one wide of his legs, and sent it an astonishing distance, in fact over the wall. Even Mr. Harwood clapped his hands, and Forrester muttered, "That's the happiest moment of his life!" Certainly Kenyon knew more about that leg-hit ever afterwards than he did at the moment, for, it must be owned, it was a fluke; but the very next ball Kenyon was out—run out through Ethel's petticoats—and the game was lost.

"Oh, Ethel!" he cried, his flush of ecstasy wiped out in an instant. "I could have run the thing myself!"

Ethel was dreadfully grieved, and showed it so unmistakably that Kenyon, shifting his ground, turned hotly to an unlucky groom who had been standing umpire.

"I don't believe she *was* out, Fisher!" he exclaimed more angrily than ever. Mr. Harwood snatched his cigar from his mouth; but C. J. forestalled his interference by running up and taking Kenyon by the arm.

"My dear fellow, I'm surprised at you! To dispute the umpire! I thought you were such a sportsman? You must learn to take a licking, and go out grinning, like a man."

Kenyon was crushed—by his hero. He stammered an apology, with a crimson face, and left the lawn with the sweetness of that leg-hit already turned in an instant to gall. And there was a knock at Forrester's door while he was dressing for dinner, and in crept Kenyon, hanging his head, and shut the door and burst into tears.

"Oh, you'll never think the same of me again, C. J.! A nice fellow you'll think me, who can't stand getting out—a nice fellow for your school!"

C. J., in his shirt and trousers, looked down very tenderly on the little quivering figure in flannels. Kenyon was standing awkwardly, as he sometimes would when tired.

"My dear old fellow, it was only a game—yet it was life! We live our lives as we play our games; and we *must* be sportsmen, and bide by the umpire's decision, and go out grinning when it's against us. Do you see, Ken?"

"I see," said Kenyon, with sudden firmness. "I have learnt a lesson. I'll never forget it."

"Ah, you may learn many a lesson from cricket, Kenyon," said C. J. "And when you have learnt to play the game—pluckily—unselfishly—as well as you can—then you've learnt how to live too!" He was only saying what he has been preaching to his school ever since; but now he says that no one has ever attended to him as Kenyon did.

Kenyon looked up with wet, pleading eyes. "Then—you will have me at St. Crispin's?"

But C. J. only ruffled the boy's brown hair.

III

A variety of hindrances prevented Forrester from revisiting Kenyon's father until August in the following year, when he arrived in the grey evening of a repulsive day. As before, he came straight from the Nottingham match; he had started his school, but was getting as much cricket as he could in the holidays. It was raining heavily when he jumped out of the carriage which had been sent to meet him. Mr. Harwood shook his hand in the cold twilight of the hall. House and host seemed silent and depressed. Forrester looked for Kenyon—for his hat, for some sign of him—as one searches for a break in the clouds.

"Where's the boy?" was his first question. "Where's Kenyon?"

"Kenyon? In bed."

"Since when?"

"The beginning of last month."

Forrester looked horrified; his manner seemed to irritate Mr. Harwood.

"Surely I wrote and told you; have you forgotten? I wrote to say he couldn't come last term, that he had fallen off during the winter, and was limping badly. Didn't you get the letter? But you did; you answered it."

"Yes, yes. I know all that," said Forrester, still bewildered. "I answered, and you never answered me. Then the term came on, and you don't know what it was. I had all my time taken up, every moment. And I have been playing cricket ever since we broke up. But—the truth is, I've been having the most cheerful letters from Kenyon all the time!"

"That's it; he *is* cheerful."

"He never said he was in bed."

"You weren't to know of it on any account. But I thought you would be prepared for it."

"Not with those letters. I can hardly believe it. Will he—won't he be able——"

"No, never; but you will find him as keen about it as ever, and as mad on cricket. He tells me, by the way, you've been doing great things yesterday—in fact I read him the report—and he's wild with delight about it. Come up and see him. You'll get another ovation."

Forrester nodded, setting his teeth. While they were conversing Ethel had entered the hall, shaken hands with him, and vanished up the shallow stairs, leaving the hall more gloomy than before. He remembered this presently; also that Ethel, in a single year, seemed changed from a child to a woman. But at the time he could see one thing only, a vision, a memory. The peculiar sadness in Mr. Harwood's tones, the tenderness which was still untender, though very different from last year's note, was yet to strike him. He could think only of Kenyon as he best remembered him, playing cricket with a sunburnt face, ardent, triumphant, angry, penitent, ashamed—and of Kenyon as he dreaded to look upon him now.

Mr. Harwood stopped on the stairs.

"I wish you could help me in one thing, Charlie. He is still counting on your school, and now he can never go. He needn't know this; but could you—I do so wish you could make him think less about it!"

Forrester coloured a little. "I wish I could," he said, thoughtfully; "and perhaps I can, for somehow I myself am less anxious to have him than I was last year. I have often been thankful he wasn't one of the boys this last term. I couldn't have borne to pitch into him as I have had to pitch into most of them. When I was here before I only looked on the pleasant side of it all.... Yes, I can tell him there's another side."

Kenyon looked a great length as he lay stretched out in bed; he seemed to have grown a good deal. His thin face was flushed with anticipation; his fine eyes burnt eagerly; he had heard the wheels in the wet gravel under his window, and C. J.'s voice in the hall and on the stairs. A thin white arm lay over the counterpane, the fingers clasping a newspaper. As Forrester entered, with a trepidation of which he was ashamed, the thin arm flourished the newspaper wildly.

"Well played, sir!" thundered Kenyon from his pillow, "Your score won the match; come and shake hands on it!"

Forrester, who had certainly troubled the Nottingham bowlers this time, was more taken aback than he had ever been on the cricket-field where astonishing things do happen. He went to the bedside and sat down there, and pressed the small boy's slender hands; but he had not a thing to say.

"The *Sportsman*," continued Kenyon, beating the bed with that paper, "says it was a fine display of cricket, and that you're in splendid form just now. So you are. Look what you did against Surrey! Do you remember how that match came *after* Notts last year, and you left here to play in it? I'm glad it was the other way round this season; and oh, I say, how glad I am you've come!"

"Dear old boy! But—look here—don't you think you might have told me you were like this, old fellow?"

Kenyon tossed his head on the pillow.

"I couldn't. It was too sickening. Besides, I thought——"

"Well?"

"You mightn't be awfully keen to come, you know."

"You needn't have thought that, Kenyon. I can't believe you did think it."

"Well, I won't swear that I did. Anyhow I didn't want you to know before you must—for lots of reasons."

Forrester let the reasons alone: he could divine one of them: the boy had hoped to be up and well before he came. Forrester wondered whether that hope held yet, and if it did, whether he honestly could share it any longer. He looked at Kenyon as he confronted this question: the flush of pleasure and excitement had subsided from the young wan face, which had now an unhealthy pallor. His face had been the best thing about Kenyon last year, the thing that inspired confidence and faith. Forrester strove to talk more cricket. Kenyon had a hundred pet cricketers, his favourites and friends on paper, whom he spoke of by their initials and knew intimately on the cricket-fields of his fancy, as formerly he had known and spoken of C. J. himself. C. J. tried to tell him of those he had met lately; but the young fellow was all distraught, he could not think of the right men, and took the newspaper to his assistance.

"So John still gets you the *Sportsman!*"

"No, John doesn't."

"You don't mean that he's left?"

"Rather not! He comes up to see me every day; the governor fetches him; and it's the governor who brings me the *Sportsman.*"

"Really?"

"Yes, and *Cricket* and the *Field,* and all the other papers that you see all over the shop."

"It's too dark to see all over the shop," said Forrester, throwing the *Sportsman* aside. "I call it very good of your father, though."

"He *is* good. He's awfully good to me since I've been lying-up, the governor. He sits with me a lot, and reads and talks to me; he reads awfully well. But he doesn't understand much about cricket, doesn't care for it. He reads me the full account of the play when I've looked at the score; but I'd as soon read them to myself if it wasn't for offending him. You see, he can't be interested, though he says he is. I should think he'd be very glad if you did it for him—if you would."

Forrester was thinking. Mr. Harwood had left him alone with Kenyon, hardly entering the room himself; he had turned away with a look which Forrester happened to see, but failed to understand. Now he had a clue: perhaps Kenyon had greeted him as he never greeted his father, that father who by the boy's own showing was trying at the last to be his friend. The thought troubled Forrester. He had been touched by a something in Mr. Harwood's manner, in the hall, on the stairs, and still more by what Kenyon had just told him; he was pleased with Kenyon's evident appreciation of his father's kindness; but—there were more buts than he could sort or separate now and here. What he did feel instantly, and acutely, was a premonition of involuntary intervention, on his own part, between father and child. In his difficulty he pushed the long brown hair from Kenyon's forehead, and looked gently into the eager eyes.

"We'll see, old fellow," he said at last; "your father mightn't quite like it, I think; and of course, as you say, you must take care not to offend him. Stick to that, Kenyon; always be good to your father and Ethel."

"They're awfully good to me, certainly," said Kenyon, with a sigh. "Dear old Ethel! Have you seen her with her hair up, C. J.?"

"I just saw her in the hall; she is quite grown up."

"She's a brick.... Do you really think the governor would mind—you reading the cricket, I mean? It *must* bore him, no matter what he says; how can it help doing?"

"It might bore him to read it to himself; it may delight him to read it to you."

Kenyon turned his cheek to the pillow, and stared at the dismal evening sky. No doubt he was wondering, in his small way, if he was a very ungrateful, unnatural son; and trying to account for it, if it was so; and wishing he were comfortably certain it was not so.

"Besides," added Forrester, "I shall not be able to stay many days, you know." Indeed it seemed to him that he had better not stay; but Kenyon's eyes were on him in a twinkling.

"How many?" he asked, almost with a gasp.

"A week at the outside; it's the Lancashire match the week after next."

Again Kenyon turned, and his sharp profile looked sharper than before against the pillow. "Of course you must play against Lancashire—and make your century," he said, with such a hollow heartiness that, first-class cricketer as he was, and few as were his present opportunities for first-class cricket, C. J. instantly resolved to cancel all remaining engagements.

Kenyon went on:

"I'm hoping to get up, you know, before long. Surely I've been here long enough? It's all rot, *I* say, keeping you in bed like this; you get as weak as a cat. I believe the governor thinks so too. I know they're going to have a doctor down from London to see me. If he lets me get up, and you come back after you've made that century, we might have some more cricket, mightn't we? I'd give anything to have some before the term begins. I want another of those leg-hits! I say, they think I might be able to go to St. Crispin's next term, don't they?"

Forrester remembered. "I don't know. You might be able, perhaps."

"Why do you say it like that?"

"Shall I tell you, old fellow? I'm not quite so keen on having you as I was a year ago. Stop! I'll tell you why. I didn't realise what it would be like. I rather fancied I should have a dozen Kenyons, and that Kenyon at school would be a saint: which was absurd, old fellow. I thought I should never, never, never lose my temper with you. Absurd again! We talked, you and I, of what we knew nothing about; *I* know something now; and it isn't all skittles and beer, Kenyon. Listen: there wasn't a fellow in the school I didn't punish time after time. Punish is a jolly word, isn't it? It would have been nice for us both, wouldn't it, my punishing you? Kenyon, there were two fellows I had to swish! You understand? I felt thankful you weren't there. I don't any longer feel that I want you there. I'd rather some other man kept you in, Kenyon, and licked you, old fellow, when you needed it." The truth is, Forrester had long had all this on his mind; as he uttered the last of it, he almost forgot why he had spoken now, and what Mr. Harwood had said on the stairs.

Kenyon lay very still, watching the darkling sky split in two by the window-sashes. He had dreamed of that school so often, he had looked forward to it so long. It was hard suddenly to stop looking forward, to have no more happy imaginary school-days from this moment forth; but if the real ones could never have been so happy, then he should feel thankful; and in any case there was less immediate necessity to be up and well, which in itself was a relief. It was sensibly darker, however, when Kenyon spoke, and once more his tone was a little forced.

"I suppose you're right. I'm glad you've told me this, C. J. I'm not so keen now, though I *have* been counting.... I suppose I couldn't even have called you C. J., eh?"

"No, you'd have had to 'sir' me."

"Indeed, sir! Then I'm thankful I'm not going, sir! There's the gong, sir, yes, sir, you must go and dress, sir! The governor'll bring you up with him to say good-night. And to-morrow—I've heaps of things to tell you to-morrow, C. J. I'll think of 'em all night—sir!"

There were tears on his eyelashes, nevertheless; but the room was now really dark; his friend could not see.

IV

Forrester's disquieting apprehension of intrusion on his part, of that cruel intervention from which he shrank, was not for long a vague sensation. Mr. Harwood himself defined it, and with startling candour, that very evening after dinner.

Forrester had described the latter part of his chat with Kenyon, the part arising from something Mr. Harwood had said on the stairs, and from that other thing which had long been in his own mind. "I wouldn't have Kenyon, now I know what it is like," he had averred, with all the earnestness he had employed upstairs.

"You wouldn't get him," said Mr. Harwood, in sad irony. "He will never be well enough, Bodley is sure, to go to school."

"Is Dr. Bodley a very good man?"

"He is a very good doctor in ordinary, so to speak; but Kenyon's case is not exactly ordinary. Bodley is getting down a London man, a specialist, for a consultation. Kenyon knows about it."

"Yes, he thought it was to see whether he might get up."

"Whether there is the least chance of his ever getting up, as a matter of fact. I don't myself think he ever will. There is some hopeless disease of the hip. An operation is the only chance, and you know what a faint one."

"I'm glad I'm here!" Forrester involuntarily exclaimed; and it was at this that Mr. Harwood had pierced him with his eye and spoken his mind.

"I am glad too," said he, slowly; "yet I am sore—God knows how sore!"

The young man moved in his chair, but did not rise. Mr. Harwood held him with his eye. Forrester leant his elbow on the table, his head against his palm, and met that bitter, pitiable, yearning gaze.

"I am glad because Kenyon wanted you so much; sore, because he wanted *you* so much. Look at the reception he gave you, ill as he is! *I* never make him like that. I might have left him for weeks, alone with Ethel and the servants, and he wouldn't have welcomed me so. Yet I am always with the boy. I do everything for him. I have been another man to him, Charlie, since you were here last year. You taught me a lesson. I don't know whether to like you or hate you for it. You taught me to be my boy's friend—at any rate to try. It wasn't easy. We tired each other—we always did—we always may. We irritate each other too: he *will* seem frightened and fight shy of me. I suppose I deserve it—God knows! We have understood each other better, we have tired each other less—I am sure—since he has been up yonder. But all the time, mark you, he has been looking forward to your coming—to going to your school in the end. About that he has talked incessantly—as if it were the one thing to get better for—and about you. You're his hero, he worships you; I am only his father. You are everything to him...."

Forrester was inexpressibly shocked and moved. "You are mistaken, believe me you are!" he cried earnestly. "He has been telling me already how good you are to him, of all you do for him."

"Ah! he is a good boy; he is very grateful. He always says 'Thank you'—to me! Heaven, how I wish he'd forget that sometimes! But no; it was in those little things that I was continually finding fault with him, and now it's his turn. He has a special manner for me. He thinks before he speaks when he speaks to me. And I see it all! Why, I stand outside the door, and hear him talking to Ethel, and when I open it his very key changes. With you it's a hundred times worse. With you—God help me!" cried Harwood, with a harsh laugh, "I'm like a child myself ... jealous of you ... for winning what I never tried nor deserved to win."

He wiped the moisture from his face, and sat cold and still.

"I'll go to-morrow!" said Forrester, hoarsely.

"You will do nothing of the kind," retorted the other in his normal voice. "You will stay as long as you like—and Kenyon needs you."

V

C. J. was early abroad next morning—as once before. The weather had cleared up in the night. Sunlight and dew did just what they had done that other morning of yester-year. Sounds and scents were the same now as then. So Forrester tried to imagine it *was* then, and to conjure Kenyon to his side. But Kenyon lay in bed behind yonder blind on the sunny side of the house, and his friend wandered desolate over last year's ground. He looked into the flagged yard where painted wickets still disfigured a certain buttress: he was sorry he had thrown cold water on "snob." On the lawn he saw other wickets, which no man had pitched, and worn places that had long been green. There was the peach-house, with the sun gleaming where once the rain had beaten an accompaniment to "Willow the King." He could hear the song—he can hear it still. Then he met John, who was visibly inconvenienced; and returning to the house, he found Ethel on the steps. She looked very fresh and beautiful, but the young man's heart was in the room upstairs, where her heart was also. A common bond of sadness drew them insensibly together. They remained there, very silent, till the gong sounded within.

Something that Mr. Harwood told him, a letter in his hand, as they sat down to breakfast, caused Forrester to run upstairs the moment they rose. Kenyon received him with grateful eyes, but with a very slight salute this morning. Sunshine flooded the room, even to the edge of the bed. Things invisible in the dusk of the previous evening caught the strong light and the eye now—the bottles, the graduated glasses, the bed-table, the framed photograph of Kenyon's mother hanging on the screen. And Kenyon himself, with the sun clasping his long brown hair, and filling the hollows of his pinched face, was a more distinct and a much more pitiful figure this morning.

"You know what's going to happen to-day, C. J.?"

"The doctors are coming—the one from London. Your father told me just before breakfast."

"Call them the umpires," said Kenyon in a queer tone. "Say they're going to give me in or out!"

Forrester made no remark. Kenyon lay watching him.

"You're perfectly right, C. J. I thought of that before. I thought of it in the night. I had time to think plenty, last night!"

"Couldn't you sleep?"

"Not a wink in the night. I've slept a little since daylight."

"Were you—you were in pain, Kenyon!"

"Don't speak of it," said Kenyon, grimly. "It was so bad that I didn't care what happened to me; and I don't care now, when I remember it. I'm thankful the doctors are coming this morning—I mean the umpires. Anything's better than last night over again. I've felt nothing like it before."

"And you never will again, old fellow! I know you won't. They'll see to that!"

"Will they?" Kenyon made a wistful pause. "So I thought up to last night: I thought they'd get me up and out again. In the night I gave up thinking so. I lay here, C. J., and asked only to be put out of my misery. I never had such a bad night before—nothing like. I've had my bad ones, but I used to grin and bear it, and think away of St. Crispin's, and you, and the fellows. But last night——"

"Well?" said C. J. in a hard voice. His heart had smitten him.

"Well, you'd made me give up the idea of St. Crispin's, you know. Don't look like that—it's just as well you did. Only I hadn't it to think about in the night. I missed it."

He shut his eyes: he *had* been thinking of St. Crispin's, but not in the old way, no longer as within his reach. Ideals are not shattered so easily by hearsay, and St. Crispin's was heaven to Kenyon still, though now he might not enter in. Well, one would rather never get there than find heaven imperfect too. And Kenyon, had he been older, would have appreciated his blessedness in being permitted to lay down this ideal unsubstantiated and as good as new; for not C. J., but experience only, could have razed so solid a castle in the air; C. J. had only lifted the drawbridge against Kenyon forever.

But Forrester was thinking of the night before.

"My dear fellow, you speak as though school were the only thing you had to live for!"

"Well, it was the thing I wanted to get better for," replied Kenyon, frankly; "one of the things anyhow. Of course I want to be up and out here as well. I love this dear old place!"

"Do you want to get strong only for your own sake?" Forrester could not help saying, gently. "Do you never think of Ethel, of your father? I am sure you do!"

Kenyon coloured.

"Don't, old fellow! It's hard to think of anybody but yourself when you're laid up in bed for weeks and weeks. But Ethel knows that I do sometimes think about her; and that reminds me, C. J.; I was going to ask you to play tennis with her, or take her out for a ride, or something. She wants to come out of her shell. And then the governor, he's so decent to me now, of course I'd like to get better for his sake too. I think he'd make less fuss about the windows now—I'd like to break another and see! But it's no good pretending I'm as sorry for them as for myself, I *can't* be."

"You are very honest," said Forrester, looking kindly into the great bright eyes. "I wish all my fellows were as brave and honest as you!"

"I'm not so brave. You don't know what I've gone through up here alone in the night, apart from the pain. I've been thinking about—it. C. J., I don't know, now, that I'm going to get better at all. I pray to, and I try to, but I don't know that I am. I say, don't hook it! I daren't say it very loud. You're the first I've said it to at all. It only came to me last night ... and it does seem hard lines. Look at the sun! With the window open like this, and your eyes shut, it's almost as good as lying out on the grass. Dear old place!... Why *have* you hooked it? What are you looking out of the window for? They can't be coming yet!"

But they were, as it happened, though that was not why Forrester had risen; nor had he answered when Kenyon heard the wheels.

"What a bother, C. J.! There was something else I meant to tell you; must you scoot? Then come up after the umpires have been, and tell me what they say—yourself. You sha'n't go till you promise!"

VI

When C. J. returned, the sun shone into the room no more; it was afternoon.

Kenyon was very white.

"Well?"

"Kenyon, they don't know!"

"But they're still in the house. Why haven't they gone? What are they waiting for? Tell me, C. J. You said you'd tell me!"

"Poor old Kenyon—dear old fellow!" faltered Forrester. "I promised to tell you, I know I did, and downstairs they've asked me to. Now you'll never feel it, Kenyon. They're going to do something which may make you better. You—you'll be put to sleep—you'll never feel a thing!"

"When is it to be?"

"This afternoon—very soon."

Kenyon drew a hard breath.

"You've got to be in the room, C. J.!"

"Very well, if they will let me. But you'll never know, Kenyon—you'll know nothing at all about it!"

"They *must* let you. You've got to hold my hand right through, whether I feel anything or not. See?"

"My dear boy! My brave old fellow!"

"It's a bargain?"

"I'd better go and ask them now."

"Hold on a bit. How you do like to do a bolt! I wish this hadn't come so soon ... there was so much I'd got to tell you ... all what I thought of in the night. You know the game we had, the night before you went, last summer? John would call it Gentlemen and Players; poor old John! I remember every bit of it—especially that leg-hit. It was sweet!. Well, when Ethel got run out, and our side lost—ah! I thought you'd remember—I played the fool, and you told me not to grumble at the umpire's decision. You said life was like cricket, and I mustn't dispute the umpire, but go out grinning———"

"I didn't mean that, Kenyon! You know I didn't! I never thought———"

"Perhaps not, but I did in the night; and I'm thinking of it now, C. J., I'm thinking of nothing else!"

VII

Kenyon had rallied: nearly a week had passed. It had done no good, but it had not killed him.

The afternoon was hot, and still, and golden. The window of Kenyon's room was wide open; it had been wide open every day. Below, on the court beyond the drive, Forrester and Ethel were playing at playing a single. Kenyon had rallied so surprisingly, and had himself begged them to play. He could not hear them, he was asleep; it was a pity; but he was sleeping continually. Mr. Harwood sat by Kenyon in the deep arm-chair. He had sent the nurse to lie down in her room. The afternoon, though brilliant, was still and oppressive.

How long he slept! Mr. Harwood seldom took his eyes from the smooth white forehead, whiter than usual under its thatch of brown hair. It was damp also, and the hair clung to it. Mr. Harwood would smooth back the hair, and actually not wake Kenyon with the sponge. His untrained fingers were grown incredibly light and tender. He would stand for minutes when he had done this, gazing down on the pale young face with the long brown locks and lashes. They were Kenyon's mother's eyelashes, as long and as dark. When Mr. Harwood raised his eyes from the boy, it was to gaze at her photograph on the screen. Kenyon in his sleep was extremely like her. The eyes in the portrait were downcast a little; they seemed to rest on Kenyon, to beckon him.

The voices of Ethel and Forrester, never loud, were audible all the time. And Mr. Harwood was glad to hear them. He did not want those two up here. He would not have Forrester up here any more; only Kenyon would. It was Forrester who had held the child's unconscious hand during the operation, and until Kenyon became sensible, when "C. J." was the first sound he uttered. There had been too much Forrester all through, much too much since the operation. It was Kenyon's doing, and Kenyon must have all his wishes now. It was not Forrester's fault. Mr. Harwood knew this, and hated Kenyon's friend the more bitterly for the feeling that another man would have loved him.

How Kenyon slept! How strange, how shallow, his breath seemed all at once! Mr. Harwood rose again, and again smoothed the long hair back from the forehead. The forehead glistened: and this time Kenyon awoke. There was a dim unseeing look in his eyes. He held out a hand, and Mr. Harwood grasped it, dropping on his knees beside the bed.

"Stick to my hand. Never let go again. Remember what you told me? *I* do—I'm thinking of it now!"

Mr. Harwood did not remember telling him any one thing. He was kneeling with his back to the window. Kenyon's sentences had come with long intervals between them, and accompanied by the most loving glances his father had ever received from him. The father's heart throbbed violently. Perhaps he realised that his boy was dying; he was more acutely conscious that Kenyon and he were alone together, and that childish love and trust had come at last into the dear, dying eyes. He had striven so hard to win this look—had longed for it of late with so mighty a longing! And at the last it was his. What else was there to grasp?

Kenyon began to murmur indistinctly—about cricket—about getting out. Mr. Harwood leant closer to catch the words, and to drink deeper while he could of the dim loving eyes. But there came suddenly a change of expression. Kenyon was silent. And Mr. Harwood never knew why.

In the garden they heard the cry, and sped into the house, and up the stairs and into the room, warm from their game. They opened the door and stood still; for they saw Kenyon as none ever had seen him before, with his face upon his father's shoulder, and a smile there such as Forrester himself had never won.

A LITERARY COINCIDENCE

It was twenty-five minutes past eight, and a fine October morning, when Mr. Wolff Mason, the popular novelist and editor of *Mayfair*, emerged from the dressing-room of his house in Kensington and came downstairs dabbing his chin with his clean pocket-handkerchief. The day had begun badly with the man of letters, whose boast it was that he had shaved for upwards of forty years without cutting himself anything like forty times. He entered the dining-room with a comically rueful expression on his kindly humorous face, and with a twitching behind the spectacles which would have led those who knew him best to prick their ears for one of the delightful things which the novelist was continually saying at his own expense. His face fell, however, when he found no one in the room but the maid who was lighting the wick beneath the plated kettle on the breakfast table.

"Has Miss Ida not come down yet?"

"Not that I know of, sir. Shall I go and see?"

"Oh, never mind, never mind," said the novelist, cursorily examining the letters on his plate, and opening none of them. "Well, upon my word, I don't know what has come over Ida," he added to himself, as he undid the fastenings of the French window which led down iron steps into the little London garden behind the house. "Yesterday morning she ran it pretty fine. The day before she was a good minute late. Of course she may be in time yet, but I do wish I could teach her to be five minutes early for everything, as I am. Ida is worse than either of her sisters in this respect; and she began by being the best of the three."

Wolff Mason sighed as he thought of his daughters. The two elder ones were married and settled, very comfortably, it is true; but if Ida followed their example, what on earth was to become of her unfortunate father? Who was to typewrite his manuscript, and correct his proofs, and peel the stamps from the enclosed envelopes of the people who wrote for the novelist's autograph? No, he could not do without Ida at any price; and Mr. Mason shook his head as he passed out into the fresh air and down the iron steps into the garden. He did more: he shook his daughters, and all creatures of mere flesh and blood, quite out of his mind.

For it was Wolff Mason's habit to spend five minutes in the garden, every morning before breakfast, when it was fine; and when it was not, to walk round the breakfast table four-and-twenty times. That filled the five minutes which he always spent in the exclusive company of the characters of his current novel. He had been heard to say that he did his day's work in those five minutes; that at the office, where he worked at his novel all the morning, he had only to sit with his pen in his hand for three hours, and fifteen hundred words of fiction was the inevitable result. That part was purely mechanical, the novelist said. He had really written it in the five minutes before breakfast. It is not generally known, however, how curiously Wolff Mason delighted in humorous depreciation of his own work and methods. One would have liked his critics to hear him on the subject; they took his writings so very much more seriously than he did himself, that they little dreamt how highly their clever elaborate reviews entertained the philosophic object of their censure. It was an open secret that Wolff Mason professed a wholesome and unaffected disregard for posterity and the critics; but if the books that delighted two generations are forgotten by a third, their writer will certainly be remembered as the most charming talker, the kindest-hearted editor, and the most methodical man of letters of his day.

To method and to habit, indeed, the novelist had been a slave all his literary life. This he admitted quite freely. On the other hand, he argued that as his habits were all good ones in themselves (with the possible exception of that ounce of tobacco which he managed to consume daily), while his methods produced a not wholly unsuccessful result, the slavery suited him very well. Certainly it was good to be five minutes early for everything, and to start most things as the clocks were striking. The dining-room clock struck the half-hour after eight as Mr. Mason re-entered and shut the French window behind him. He had thought out the half-chapter for that day with even more than his customary minute prevision. This was all very good indeed. It was bad, however, that he should find himself now quite alone in the room, with the hot plates and the bacon growing cold, the kettle steaming furiously over the thin blue flame, and no Ida to make the tea.

Mr. Mason took up his position with an elbow on the mantel-piece and one foot to the fire, and stared solemnly at the clock. It was a worse case than yesterday. Two, three, four minutes passed. Then there was a rustle in the hall; light, quick footsteps ran across the room, and a nervous little hand was laid upon the novelist's shoulder. In another instant he was looking down into great dark eyes filled with the liveliest contrition, and making a mental note of the little black crescents underneath.

"Dear father, can you forgive me?"

"I'll try to, my dear, since you look so—penitent."

He had been about to say "pale." As he kissed the girl's cheek, its pallor was indeed conspicuous. As a rule she had the loveliest colour, which harmonised charmingly with the sweet clear brown of her eyes and hair. Ida

Mason was in fact a very beautiful and graceful girl, but lately she had grown thin and quiet, and the salt was gone out of her in many subtle ways which did not escape the spectacles of that trained observer, her father. Mr. Mason glanced over the *Times* while his tea was being made, and knew all that was in it before his cup was poured out, the bacon on his plate, and the toast-rack set within easy reach of his hand.

"A singularly dull paper," said he, as he flung it aside and Ida sat down.

"Yes?"

"It is absolutely free from news. At this time of year there's more fun in the papers that lend themselves to egregious contributions from the public. I see, however, that Professor Palliser died last night——"

"How dreadful!"

"In his ninety-third year," added Mr. Mason, dryly, to his own sentence.

"I'm afraid I was thinking of someone else," said Ida lamely.

"Of me, my dear? Then I *will* take another piece of sugar, if you don't object. The fact is, you didn't give me any at all. No, that's the salt!"

Ida laughed nervously. "I am so stupid this morning! Please forgive me, dear father."

"I hope there is nothing the matter?"

"Nothing at all."

"That's right. I fear that the religious novel is to have a most undesirable vogue. The *Times* reviews three in one column. We have to thank 'Robert Elsmere' for this."

"And 'Humphry Ward, Preacher,'" suggested Ida.

The novelist arched his eyebrows and bent forward over his plate. "Exactly," said he, after a slight pause. He did not look at his daughter. Otherwise he would have seen that she was eating nothing, and that her eyes were full of tears. It was plain to him, however, that for some reason or other, into which it was not his business to inquire, it would be unkind to press further conversation upon Ida, whom he merely thanked more affectionately than usual for moving his plate and for pouring out his second cup of tea. Over breakfast the novelist always took half an hour precisely. The clock was striking nine when he rose from the table and went upstairs to take leave of his wife.

Mrs. Mason was a sweet, frail woman of sixty, who for years had breakfasted in her own room. Without being actually an invalid, she owed it to her quiet mornings upstairs that she was still able to see her friends in the afternoon, and to dine out at moderate intervals. For five-and-thirty years his wife had been Wolff Mason's guardian angel. On her wedding-day she had been just as proud of her unknown bridegroom as she was now of the celebrated *littérateur*, and had loved the stalwart young fellow of eight-and-twenty only less dearly than the white old man of sixty-three. He found her with her tea and toast growing cold on the bed-table at her side; she was reading Ida's typewritten copy of the novel upon which he himself was then engaged.

"My dear Wolff," Mrs. Mason exclaimed, greeting her husband with the enthusiastic smile which had inspired and consoled him in the composition of so many works of fiction, "I am delighted with these last chapters! You have never done better: you might have written the love scenes thirty years ago. But you look put out, dear Wolff. Have they been stupid downstairs?"

"We are all stupid to-day, including my dear wife if she really thinks much of my love scenes. I cut myself shaving, to begin with. Then Ida was late for breakfast—four long minutes late—and for the third time this week. I *am* put out, and it's about Ida. It is not only that she is late, but there are rings under her eyes, and she forgets the sugar in your tea, and when you ask for it hands you the salt, and when you speak to her she answers inanely. She pulled a long face when I told her that Professor Palliser died last night, though the poor dear old gentleman has been on a public death-bed these eighteen months. She came a fearful howler over a book which she herself has read, to my knowledge, within the last fortnight. For the life of me I can't think what ails her."

"Can you not?"

Mrs. Mason had put down the typewritten sheets, and lay gazing at her husband with gentle shrewdness in her kind eyes.

"No, I cannot," said the novelist, defiantly.

"Have you quite forgotten Saltburn-by-the-Sea?"

"I am certainly doing my best to forget it, my dear; a deadlier fortnight I never spent in my life. Not a decent library in the place, nor a man in the hotel who knew more than the mere alphabet of whist! Why remind me of it, my love?"

"Because that's what ails Ida. She is suffering from the effects of Saltburn-by-the-Sea."

"My dear Margaret, I simply don't believe it!"

"But I know it, Wolff. Do listen to reason. Dear Ida has told me everything, and I am sorry to say she is very sadly in love."

"In love with whom?" cried the novelist, who had been pacing up and down the room, after the manner of his kind, but who stopped now at the foot of the bed, to spread his hands out eloquently. "With that young Overton?"

"With that young Over*man*. You were so short and sharp with him, you see, that you never even mastered his name."

"I was naturally short and sharp with a young fellow whom she had only seen two or three times in her life—once on the pier, once in the gardens, once or twice about the hotel. It was a piece of confounded presumption! We didn't even know who or what the fellow was!"

"He put you in the way of finding out, and you said you didn't want to know."

"No more I did," said Wolff Mason.

"You liked him well enough before he proposed to Ida."

"That may be. He had more idea of whist than any of the others, which is saying precious little. But his proposal was a piece of infernal impertinence, and I told him so."

"I am sorry you told him so, Wolff," said Mrs. Mason softly. "However, the affair is quite a thing of the past. You put a stop to it pretty effectually, and I daresay it was for the best. Only it is right you should know that young Overman and Ida met in Oxford Street yesterday, and that she has not slept all night for thinking about him."

"The villain!" cried Wolff Mason, excitedly. "I suppose he asked her to run away with him?"

"They did not speak. I was with Ida," said his wife. "It was the purest accident. Ida bowed—indeed, so did I—and he took off his hat, but no one stopped or spoke. Ida is troubled because he looked extremely wretched; even I can see his eyes now as they looked when we passed him. However, as I say, you put a stop to the matter, and they must both get over it as best they can. I have never blamed you, I think. It *was* very premature, I grant you. My only feeling has been that, as a writer of romance all your days, you showed remarkably little sympathy with a pair of sufficiently romantic young lovers!"

"My dear, I choose to keep romance in its proper place—between the covers of my books. I have more than enough of it there, I can assure you, if I could afford to consult my own taste."

"You can't put in too much of it to suit mine. Your love-story has been the strong point in all your novels, Wolff, and it is still. This new one is of your very best in that respect. I foresee a sweet scene in the boat-house."

"I am in the middle of it now," the novelist said, complacently.

"I have visions of the old general turning up when she is in his arms. I do hope you won't let him, Wolff."

"How well you know my work, my love! The general came in and caught them just before I wiped my pen yesterday. It ended the chapter very nicely. I was in good form at lunch."

"And what is going to happen to-day?"

"Can you ask? The general blusters. George behaves like a gentleman, and scores all down the line, for the time being."

"But surely she is allowed to marry him in the end?"

"She always is, my dear, in my books."

Mrs. Mason cast upon her husband a fixed look which turned slowly into a sweet, grave smile. He was still standing at the foot of the bed, but now he was leaning on the brass rail, with his hands folded quietly, and a good-humoured twinkle in his eyes.

Whatever he might say about his own books at the club, he enjoyed chatting them over with his wife as keenly as in the dear early days when his first book and their eldest daughter appeared simultaneously. He had forgotten Ida for the moment, and the pleasant though impossible young man at the sea-side; but Mrs. Mason did not mean that moment to be prolonged.

"Ah," said she, "in your books! Twice you have allowed the heroine to marry the hero in your life too."

"I was under the impression, my dear, that we were talking about my books."

"But I am thinking about Ida. You needn't look at the clock, Wolff. You know very well that you never leave the house before ten minutes past, and it isn't five past yet. You may look at your watch if you like, but you will see that my clock is, if anything, fast. I say that you raised no opposition in the case of either Laura or Hetty."

"Didn't I?" exclaimed the novelist with a grim chuckle. "By Jove, I did my worst! If that wasn't very bad you must remember that we knew all about Charles and Macfarlane. It wasn't like young Overton. By Jove, no!"

"Young Overman's is better romance," murmured Mrs. Mason.

"Therefore, it is worse real life. I do wish you would see with me that the two things clash if you try to bring them together. Frankly, my dear, I wish you wouldn't try. I make a point of never doing so—that's why I don't live over the shop."

"Wolff, Wolff, say that sort of thing at your club! With me you can afford to be sincere. Why, you have put Ida's hair and eyes into every book you have written since she grew up. The things don't clash. If you borrow from Ida for your books, I think you ought to be prepared to pay her back out of your books too, and allow her to live happily ever after, like all the rest of your heroines."

There were moments when Wolff Mason realised that the one-sided game of letters has a bad effect on the argumentative side of a man's mind. The present was one. He looked again at his watch, and replaced it very hurriedly in his waistcoat pocket.

"My dear, I really must be going."

"One minute more—just one," pleaded Mrs. Mason, and her voice was as soft as ever it had been thirty years ago. "I want your hand, Wolff!"

The novelist came round to the bedside and sat down for a few moments on the edge. During those few moments two frail, worn, thin hands were joined together, and Wolff Mason's spectacles showed him a moisture in his wife's eyes—not tears, but a shining film which only made them more lovely and sweet and kind. That film had come over them in the old days when they were both young and he had told her of his love. On very rare occasions he had described it in the eyes of his dark-eyed heroines, and never without a hotness in his own. He rose suddenly. His hand was pressed.

"You will reconsider it, Wolff?"

"My dear, she is our last."

"My love, we have each other!"

Some moments later, when Wolff Mason had closed the door behind him, he had to open it again to hear what it was that his wife was calling after him.

"Mind you don't make the general *too* inhuman, Wolff, or I shall be so disappointed in you both!"

The novelist laughed. So did his wife. The secret of their complete happiness was not love alone. It was love and laughter.

Nevertheless, Wolff Mason drove to the office of the *Mayfair Magazine* in a less literary frame of mind than he either liked or was addicted to at this early hour of the day. It is not true that the novelist constructed all his stories in the hansom which deposited him in Paternoster Row at a quarter to ten every morning, and in front of his own door at a quarter-past seven in the evening. That was the invention of the lady journalists who wrote paragraphs about Wolff Mason for the evening papers—those paragraphs his old-world soul abhorred. It is a fact, however, that he liked to get out of his hansom with more ideas than he had taken into it. He made it a rule to think only of his work on the drive in.

But this morning he was breaking all his rules: he had cut himself with his razor; he had left the house five minutes late, owing to a series of little domestic scenes of which his head was still full. And how he hated scenes outside his books! He treated the psychological moments in his own life as lightly, indeed, as in his novels, but the former worried him. This morning he had kissed Mrs. Mason with all the exuberance of a young man, and on coming downstairs, and finding Ida waiting for him with his tall hat and overcoat nicely brushed, and his gloves warmed on both sides, he had kissed her too, and so fondly as to bring out the same film on her sweet eyes as he had produced a few minutes before in those of her mother.

To begin the day by making people cry was peculiarly odious to the kind-hearted gentleman who held it the whole duty of a novelist to make people laugh; and those two pairs of dear eyes, so like each other in every look, duly accompanied him to the orderly, tobacco-scented room, where he edited *Mayfair* and wrote his own books. The clock on the chimney-piece stood at ten minutes to ten. He was five minutes late at this end also.

On a little table under the window lay the long envelopes and the cylinders of manuscript which had arrived since the day before. Wolff Mason lit a cigarette, and examined the packets without opening them. Thus he invariably began his official day, tossing aside the less interesting-looking missives for his weekly "clean sweep," and leaving on the little table work enough for the afternoon, mostly the work of previously accepted contributors, whose handwriting was familiar to the editor. These were the people who gave the trouble, the people who had sent in a good thing once. Not all of them did it twice.

The editor recognised this morning on one of the long envelopes the superscription of a most promising contributor who had done it thrice, but who had lately failed as many times in succession. Wolff Mason had never known a valued contributor go to the bad at such a pace; but this one had done such merry work in the beginning that there was hope for him still. At all events he could write, and must therefore be read carefully. The editor would have read him there and then, in the hope of a laugh, which he felt he needed, had he not been five minutes late as it was. At three minutes to ten he loaded four brier-wood pipes out of a stone tobacco-jar, set three of them in a row on his desk, and lit the fourth. When the hour struck the ink stood thick on certain symbols at the top of a clean sheet of unlined foolscap, and Wolff Mason was glancing over his previous morning's work.

The clock on the chimney-piece had a quiet, inoffensive tick, but this, and an occasional squeal from the novelist's pipe, which was exceedingly foul, were the only sounds within the editorial sanctum between ten and half-past that morning. The ink had dried upon the pen of as ready a writer as ever told agreeable stories in good English; at the half-hour all that had been written was the heading of the new chapter, and the number of the page (with a ring round it) in the right-hand top corner. Some ten minutes later Wolff Mason took up his second pipe, lit it, and began to write. He wrote for an hour, more rapidly and less gracefully than was his wont. Then he flung down his pen, lit the third pipe, and blew clouds of smoke against the square of blue framed by the upper sashes of the double window on his right. The novelist was in trouble. The best character in his book, the old general, was failing him sadly in the hour of need. It was necessary to the plot that this hearty, weather-beaten warrior should make a complete brute of himself in the boat-house on discovering his only daughter in the embrace of the young poet who inhabited cheap chambers in Mitre Court when he was at home. But the general had treated the poet as his own son hitherto, had taken his daughter to tea at the Mitre Court chambers, had himself invited their interesting tenant down to his country house for change of air; and he refused to be so inconsistent. It was a case of inventing something disreputable (afterwards to be disproved) against the poet; the general must only now have heard of it to justify his ordering his guest off the premises as the plot demanded. It was necessary and easy, but undeniably conventional, and it distressed the novelist, because he had not foreseen this contingency in the garden before breakfast. Moreover, for some reason or other, he felt his inventive faculty to be at its lowest vitality to-day. He did not ask himself what the reason was. He had at least got back to the world of fiction, and whatever their effects, the domestic scenes of the early morning were entirely forgotten.

He was aware, however, that this morning he was breaking all his rules. He was about to invent in the room where it was his practice only to write down what he had invented elsewhere. He got up and paced the room in order to do so, and this was another rule broken, for he very seldom stirred from his chair between ten o'clock and one. And now, as he walked, Wolff Mason's eye was caught by the packet from that promising contributor who could write so amusingly when he liked; the creative portion of his brain gave sudden way to the editorial; and the editor informed himself, with a characteristic chuckle of self-depreciation, that the new man's story would in any case amuse him more than his own was doing at the moment. At all events he would try it. He had broken so many rules already that he caught up the interesting envelope with a certain recklessness, and having lighted his fourth pipe, sat down to read manuscript as calmly as though it were three o'clock in the afternoon instead of the middle of his sacred working morning.

The story, which was quite short, was accompanied by the unpresuming business-like note which this contributor always forwarded with his literary offerings. It was called "A Good Father," which was not a very good title, but the editor prepared to give it his "careful consideration," in accordance with the pledge embodied in his printed notice to contributors. He pushed his spectacles on to his forehead and began to read with the manuscript held close to his nose. Over the third leaf his fine, thoughtful forehead became scored with furrows; on the fifth he exclaimed "Ha!" Half way through the story he muttered "Upon my word!" and a little later, "A most remarkable coincidence." Then his face lost its interested look under the gathering clouds of disappointment, and he finished reading with a brow awry.

"Not free from merit—anything but free—yet it won't do! This is a young man with a naturally sweet sense of humour, but something has embittered him since he first began to send me his stories. I wish I knew what! He is the most disappointing person I have had to deal with for many a day; a writer after my own heart, which he is half breaking with his accursed childish cynicism!"

The genuine character of the editor's regrets was obvious (to himself) from the fact that all his observations were made aloud. He very seldom caught himself in the act of soliloquy; it was yet another of the several irregularities which were destined to stamp this day in the memory of one who notoriously lived and worked by routine. The matter of the unacceptable story, however, suggested an entry in the commonplace book in which he was accustomed to accumulate raw material for future use. He felt happier when he had jotted down a note or two anent the cynicism of the modern young author and his lamentable liking for unhappy endings. The story he had just read ended shockingly, and all owing to the unnatural obduracy of an impossible parent, the "Good Father" of the cynical title. Otherwise it was a very good story indeed. The coincidence, however, was quite remarkable. Paternal opposition was the rock on which Wolff Mason's own pen had split that morning. But his old general was not going to run him into an unhappy ending—not he! He turned to that irate personage with positive relief, and saw his way more clearly after the ten minutes he had spent in the company of a much more terrible specimen of the same class. What he did not see was the full force of the coincidence which had caused him to exclaim aloud. It was a double one; but the man of letters lived a double life, and in the atmosphere of fiction had forgotten those unpleasant facts which had compelled his attention earlier in the day.

Another matter worried the writer when the clock struck one, and he found himself mechanically wiping the pen that had inscribed some twelve hundred and fifty words only instead of the regulation fifteen hundred. He felt humbled by a sense of failure most mortifying at his age, and though he put away his papers and went off to the club as usual, he was not in his customary spirits, and the younger novelists who listened for his good things, in order to repeat them to their friends, heard nothing worth taking home with them that day. One of the latter, indeed, broached very deftly the subject of Wolff Mason's books; but the veteran treated the subject with unnatural seriousness, was aware of the unnaturalness himself, and left the club before his time in an evil humour. And evil humours were the greatest rarity of all with the editor of the *Mayfair*, whom common consent credited with the most charming personality in literary London.

By two-thirty he was back in the editorial chair; the first of a newly-loaded set of pipes was in full blast under his nose, and the remaining contents of the little table under the window were being dealt with carefully and in turn. Not one of them proved to be of any use at all. In each case this kind-hearted man felt it his duty to pen a considerate little letter explaining the reason of rejection in the present instance, and encouraging the unsuccessful contributor to further effort. It is amazing, indeed, and little known, what a talent Wolff Mason had for the composition of kindly little notes of this nature; he made even the rejected love him, for his heartening words, and for the sympathy and humour with which he tempered disappointment to his tender young contributors.

Last of all this afternoon he returned to "A Good Father," and glanced over it again with a sigh. Then he took a sheet of *Mayfair Magazine* note-paper, and scrawled the date and "Dear Sir." There he stopped. After a few moments' hesitation, the spoilt sheet was dropped into the waste-paper basket, and a new note begun with "My" thrown in before the "Dear Sir." But the editor paused again.

"Confound the fellow," he cried at last, "I'll treat him as a friend! The chances are he'll turn and rend me; but here goes."

The note that was eventually written and posted ran as follows:—

"Dear Mr. Evan Evans,—I think that 'A Good Father' is excellent, but on the whole it does not strike me as being in your best style—which is capital. If I may be permitted to make an unofficial observation, you will, I think, pardon the expression of an old man's regret that a writer with a real sense of humour, like yourself, should subordinate it to what strikes one as an alien melancholy. If you would only write as cheerfully as you did some time back, I should be spared the disappointment of returning your MS., which I shall never do without peculiar and personal regrets.

"Yours very truly,

"WOLFF MASON."

The good editor breathed more freely when he had got this letter off his mind, and had addressed it to Evan Evans, Esq., 17, Cardigan Mansions, Kensington, W., and closed the envelope with his own hand and tongue. It was his last act at the office that day. As he tossed the letter into one basket, and the rejected manuscript into another, the clock on the chimney-piece struck the half-hour after four. And at half-past four in the afternoon, summer and winter, seed-time and harvest, with the annual exception of a hateful holiday at some such place as Saltburn, the editor of the *Mayfair Magazine* returned to his club to play whist for an hour and a half precisely, with three kindred spirits as methodical and as enthusiastic as himself.

But this was the exceptional day which proved every rule of Wolff Mason's most ruly life by causing him to break each of them in turn. He played his cards towards evening as amateurishly as he had chosen his phrases in the forenoon. Now what is about to be written down may never be believed. But at five-thirty-three, by the card-room clock, Wolff Mason, who was more eminent among the few as a whist-player than as a writer of novels, put the last trump on his partner's thirteenth card. One has it on unimpeachable authority. A few minutes later the rubber came to an end, and, instead of playing out time, as the custom was with this sporting quartette, the novelist complained of a slight faintness (which explained everything) and left the club twenty minutes before six for the first time for many years.

One of the other three saw him into his hansom. He said that the air entirely revived him. It might have done so, if there had ever been anything the matter with him. He ailed nothing, however, beyond extreme and cumulative mortification; and the four winds of heaven, chasing each other round his temples as he drove westward, could not have blown that cobweb out of his respected head.

He could no longer feel surprised at anything that he might do, or say, or think. Somewhere in the neighbourhood of the park he managed to think upon Evan Evans's latest story, now on its way back to that uneven contributor, and it seemed only natural that the shrewdest, most experienced magazine-editor in London should question the wisdom of his late decision in a way that would have made him laugh on any other occasion. He did not laugh now. The optimist of letters was in an incredibly pessimistic mood, in which the story he had refused seemed to him an ideal one for the magazine. He thought of his valued and most promising contributor, Evan Evans, of the manuscript now on its way back to him, of the possible effect of the rejection of so good a story upon a sensitive young man with a knowledge of other markets. Then he thought of this contributor's address, which was quite close to his own, and of the twenty minutes which he had in hand owing to his premature departure from the club. A word on the spur to the cab-man, a sharp turn to the left, some easy driving along a quiet street, and the hansom pulled up before the respectable portals of Cardigan Mansions, Nos. 11-22, whereof the stout attendant in uniform came forward and threw back the panels.

In another minute Wolff Mason was pressing the electric bell outside No. 17 on the second floor, and reflecting, with a qualm, that he was about to intrude upon a rejected contributor whom he had never seen—a truly startling reversal of a far too common editorial experience of his own. An elderly servant opened the door.

"Is Mr. Evans at home?"

"Mr. Hevans, sir?"

The servant looked as vacant as a woman need.

"Mr. Evan Evans," said the editor, distinctly, and with a smile as it struck him that there was no occasion in the world for him to leave his name. But a light had broken over the crass face of the elderly door-opener.

"Oh, I know, sir! He *is* in. Will you step this way?"

There was no drawing back now. Mr. Mason stepped boldly across the threshold, and the door closed behind him. In the very narrow passage the servant squeezed by him, and paused with her fingers on the handle of a door upon the right-hand side.

"What name shall I say, sir?"

"Mr. Wolff Mason."

A moment later the novelist-editor found himself standing in a more charming study than he himself owned to that day. It was all books and pictures, and weapons and pretty curtains, and comfortable chairs and handy tables. A good fire was burning, and on the right of it was a desk so placed that the writer looked out into the room as he sat at his work. The writer was sitting there now. He was a very young man, with a pipe in his mouth and a pen in his hand, and as he leant forward with the utmost eagerness, and the light of his writing-lamp fell full upon his youthful face, Wolff Mason had not the slightest difficulty in recognising Ida's presumptuous suitor of Saltburn-by-the-Sea.

"How do you do, Mr. Mason?" the young fellow said, coming forward with his hand frankly outstretched; but the other hesitated before taking it in his.

"Am I speaking to Mr. Evan Evans?"

"That is the name I—write stories under."

"Exactly. Your other name is not my concern. I don't seek to know it, Mr. Evans."

The editor was smiling grimly, but his gloved hand was now extended. Now, however, that of the young man went coolly into his trousers' pocket as he looked his visitor steadily in the face. They were grey flannel trousers, with yellow slippers at one end of them and a Norfolk jacket at the other. The editor's smile had turned to a look of interest.

"I called to see you about a little story, Mr. Evans."

"You have done me a very great honour, sir. Won't you sit down? Do you find it warm? Shall I open the window?"

"Not at all, not at all. I won't detain you a moment, and I won't sit down in one of your chairs, because they look comfortable, and I am stiff—though you wouldn't think it from my breaking in upon you like this, would you?"

Having shown very plainly that it was not his intention to recognise any former acquaintance, and seeing his young host take the cue from him in a way that struck him as at once manly and gentlemanly, Mr. Wolff Mason was now behaving in his own most charming fashion, which was very charming indeed to a young unknown beginner from a favourite old author whose name had been a household word for a quarter of a century at least. The beginner felt that if he had gauged the character of Wolff Mason correctly, when they first met at the sea-side, he would never have concealed the identity of Jack Overman with Evan Evans. But all thought of the old man's hardness upon a young one perished in an overwhelming sense of the great editor's kindness towards his utterly unknown contributor.

"I'll stand here, if I may, with my back to your fire. I looked in about the very clever little story you sent me yesterday."

The young author's face brightened till it quivered, but his words were all unworthy.

"How awfully kind of you!"

"Not at all, my dear sir. I was passing close to you, on my way home, and I was bothering about your story. I admire your work, but I don't altogether admire this story. My dear fellow, it ends too sadly altogether!"

"No other ending was possible," the young man declared. "So I felt, and one must write as one feels."

"Must one?" said the veteran, smiling blandly into the boyish earnest face. "Surely all things are possible to him who writes—unless, to be sure, he takes himself seriously!"

This, however, was not very seriously said, for Wolff Mason had turned round and was peering at the photographs on and over the mantel-piece. Suddenly he pushed up his spectacles and thrust his head close to a framed portrait, with a piece of stamp-paper stuck upon the glass to hide the face, but with the name in print underneath upon the mount.

"May I ask, young man," inquired Mr. Mason, as he favoured his contributor with a very comical stare, "why you have my photograph on the wall, in the first place; and, in the second, why the deuce you cover up my face?"

"You must ask the man who lives with me. He may come in any moment now."

"Did he do it?"

"I'm ashamed to say he did."

"Upon my word I should like to know why!"

"Well, sir, he bought me your photograph when you were accepting my stories; and he hid your face because he said——"

"Well, what did he say?"

"He talked such rot, sir!"

"I have no doubt."

"He was ass enough to say you'd certainly live to hide it yourself on my account! I'm afraid that he unduly admires my stuff. He's a fellow who is full of sympathy——"

"And not free from humour—by no means free!" cried Mr. Mason, laughing at the top of his voice (as he had never, never laughed at Saltburn-by-the-Sea). "But seriously, you are ending your later stories far too sadly. To come back to your last one—though I'm afraid it's coming back to you! I rejected it, and then, as I was driving home, I thought you would perhaps alter it, if I called and asked you before you sent it elsewhere. Don't you think you could soften your good father—just at the end?"

"I couldn't," said the young fellow, with a candid stare; but his eyes fell under the cool, kindly scrutiny of the elderly man, who continued gazing at the well-shaped head, on which the hair was perhaps a trifle long and untidy. For once that day Wolff Mason was the equal of the occasion, and he knew it to his consolation. The occasion, moreover, was the very one to which he would have desired to rise.

"Why couldn't you, my dear fellow?"

"Because it isn't life."

"Are you so sure that you know life?"

"I know it as I find it," said the young fellow bitterly; and there was a pause.

"Well, at any rate, you know that I like your stories."

"I am thankful to hear it."

"I want to accept them——"

"You are very kind."

"As many of them as ever you can write, and some day a long novel. I believe in you, Overton."

"Oh, sir, you are more than kind—to a raw recruit—on the ladder which you yourself——"

"My good Overton, why on earth didn't you mix those metaphors three months ago? Not that you're raw at all—unless it's with me!"

Two frail hands were laid on the young man's shoulders. He answered dryly:

"My other name isn't Overton. It's Over*man*. But I forgot, you said it wasn't your concern!"

"Ah, well, but the man who is to make the name famous is becoming my very grave concern. You should have let me know that you were in our swim, my boy."

"Before I was sure of keeping myself afloat? I thought I had a better chance as a—bad whist-player!"

"Confound the boy!" cried Wolff Mason, "but you were perfectly right, though your work is better than your whist."

"Then it was your magazine that I was writing for—you were the one man in England who could help me on—the whole situation was so liable to misconstruction!"

"It was—it was. And, now I think of it, you never brought me an introduction nor asked for an interview, nor wrote me a single superfluous line!"

"I wanted you to accept my stuff," said the young fellow, smiling.

But behind his spectacles the editor's eyes sparkled for an instant with something more than human kindness. He had made the grand discovery of his editorial life. He had discovered the ideal contributor, and for the moment he could only think of him as a young man of letters. Now, however, his right hand had found its way into that of young Overman, as he said with a comic solemnity:

"Look here, Overton, I was five minutes late in leaving the house this morning; for once in a way I don't mind if I'm five minutes late in getting back. I think that all you need do is to shave, though Ida might prefer you in another pair of bags and slippers. You can't improve upon that Norfolk jacket—but—but you and I must have another talk about the end of your story."

"AUTHOR! AUTHOR!"

This story has to do with two men and a play, instead of a woman, and it is none of mine. I had it from an old gentleman I love: only he ought to have written it himself. This, however, he will never do, having known intimately in his young days one of the two men concerned. But I have his leave to repeat the story more or less as he told it—if I can. And I am going to him for my rebuke—when I dare.

"You want to hear the story of poor old Pharazyn and his play? I'm not going to tell it you....

"Ah, well! My recollection of the matter dates from one summer's night at my old rooms in the Adelphi, when he spoilt my night's work by coming in flushed with an idea of his own. I remember banging the drawer into which I threw my papers to lock them away for the night; but in a few minutes I had forgotten my unfinished article, and was glad that Pharazyn had come. We were young writers, both of us; and, let me tell you, my good fellow, young writing wasn't in those days what it is now. I am thinking less of merit than of high prices, and less of high prices than of cheap notoriety. Neither of us had ever had our names before the public—not even in the bill of an unread and unreadable magazine. No one cared about names in my day, save for the half-dozen great ones that were then among us; so Pharazyn's and mine never got into the newspapers, though some of them used our stuff.

"In a manner we were rivals, for we were writing the same sort of thing for the same sort of publications, and that was how we had come together; but never was rivalry friendlier, or mutually more helpful. Our parts were strangely complementary: if I could understand for the life of me the secret of collaboration, I should say that I might have collaborated with Pharazyn almost ideally. I had the better of him in point of education, and would have turned single sentences against him for all he was worth; and I don't mind saying so, for there my superiority ended. When he had a story to tell he told it with a swing and impetus which I coveted him, as well I might to this day; and if he was oftener without anything to write about, his ideas would pay twenty shillings in the pound, in strength and originality, where mine made some contemptible composition in pence. That is why I have been a failure at fiction—oh, yes, I have! That is why Pharazyn would have succeeded, if only he had stuck to plain ordinary narrative prose.

"The idea he was unable to keep within his own breast, on the evening of which I am telling you, was as new, and simple, and dramatic as any that ever intoxicated the soul of story-teller or made a brother author green with envy. I can see him now, as I watched him that night, flinging to and fro with his quick, nervous stride, while he sketched the new story—bit by bit, and often the wrong bit foremost; but all with his own flashing vividness, which makes me so sorry—so sorry whenever I think of it. At moments he would stand still before the chair on which I sat intent, and beat one hand upon the other, and look down at me with a grand, wondering smile, as though he himself could hardly believe what the gods had put into his head, or that the gift was real gold, it glittered so at first sight. On that point I could reassure him. My open jealousy made me admire soberly. But when he told me, quite suddenly, as though on an afterthought, that he meant to make a play of it and not a story, I had the solid satisfaction at that moment of calling him a fool.

"The ordinary author of my day, you see, had a certain timorous respect for the technique of the stage. It never occurred to us to make light of those literary conventions which it was not our business to understand. We were behind you fellows in every way. But Pharazyn was a sort of forerunner: he said that any intelligent person could write a play, if he wanted to, and provided he could write at all. He said his story was a born play; and it was, in a way; but I told him I doubted whether he could train it up with his own hand into a good acting one. I knew I was right. He had neither the experience nor the innate constructive faculty, one or other of which is absolutely necessary for the writing of possible plays. I implored him to turn the thing into a good dramatic novel, and so make his mark at one blow. But no; the wilful fit was on him, and one had to let it run its course. Already he could see and hear his audience laughing and crying, so he said, and no doubt he had further visions of his weekly cheque. Anyhow, we sat up all night over it, arguing, smoking, and drinking whisky until my windows overlooking the river caught the rising sun at an angle. Then I gave in, for poor old Pharazyn was more obstinate than ever, though he thanked me with the greatest good temper for my well-meant advice.

"'And look here, my boy,' says he, as he puts on his hat, 'you shan't hear another word about this till the play's written; and you are to ask no questions. Is that a bargain? Very well, then. When I've finished it—down to the very last touches—*you* shall come and sit up all night with *me*, and I'll read you every word. And by George, old chap, if they give me a call the first night, and want a speech—and I see you sitting in your stall, like a blessed old fool as you are—by George, sir, I'll hold up you and your judgment to the ridicule of the house, so help me Himmel!'

"Well, I am coming to that first night presently. Meanwhile, for the next six months I saw very little of Pharazyn, and less still in the new year. He seldom came to my rooms now; when he did I could never get him to stay and sit up with me; and once when I climbed up to his garret (it was literally that) he would not answer me, though I could smell his pipe through the key-hole in which he'd turned the key. Yet he was perfectly friendly whenever we did meet. He said he was working very hard, and indeed I could imagine it; his personal appearance, never his strong point, being even untidier, not to say seedier, than of old. He continued to send me odd magazines in which his stuff happened to appear, or, occasionally a proof for one's opinion and suggestions; we had done this to each other all along; but either I did not think about it, or somehow he led me to suppose that his things were more or less hot from the pen, whereas many of mine had been written a twelve-month before one saw them in type. One way or another I gathered that he was at work in our common groove, and had shelved, for the present at all events, his proposed play, about which you will remember I had undertaken to ask no questions.

"I was quite mistaken. One night in the following March he came to me with a haggard face, a beaming eye, and a stout, clean manuscript, which he brought down with a thud on my desk. It was the play he had sketched out to me eight or nine months before. I was horrified to hear he had been at work upon it alone from that night to this. He actually boasted that he hadn't written another line in all that time, only each line of his play some ten times over.

"I recollect looking curiously at his shabby clothes, and then reminding him that it was at his place, not mine, I was to have heard him read the play: and how he confessed that he had no chair for me there—that his room was practically dismantled—that he had sacrificed everything to the play and would do so again. I was extremely angry. I could have helped him so easily, independent as I was of the calling I loved to follow. But there was about him always an accursed unnecessary independence, which has since struck me—and I think I may say so after all these years—as the mark of a rather humble, deadly honest origin.

"He read me the play, and I cried over the third act, and so did he. I thought then, and still think, that there was genius in that third act—it took you off your feet. And to me, certainly, it seemed as if the piece must act as well as it read, though indeed, as I took care to say and to repeat, my opinion was well-nigh valueless on that point. I only knew that I could see the thing playing itself, as I walked about the room (for this time I was the person who was too excited to sit still), and that was enough to make one sanguine. I became as enthusiastic about it as though the work were mine (which it never, never would or could have been), yet I was unable to suggest a single improvement, or to have so much as a finger-tip in the pie. Nor could I afterwards account for its invariable reception at the hands of managers, whose ways were then unknown to me. That night we talked only of one kind of reception. We were still talking when once more the sun came slanting up the river to my windows; you could hardly see them for tobacco-smoke, and this time we had emptied a bottle to the success of Pharazyn's piece.

"Oh, those nights—those nights once in a way! God forgive me, but I'd sacrifice many things to be young again and feel clever, and to know the man who would sit up all night with me to rule the world over a bottle of honest grog. In the light of after events I ought perhaps to be ashamed to recall such a night with that particular companion. But it is ridiculous, in my opinion, to fit some sort of consequence to every little solitary act; and I shall never admit that poor Pharazyn's ultimate failing was in any appreciable degree founded or promoted by those our youthful full-souled orgies. I know very well that afterwards, when his life was spent in waylaying those aforesaid managers, in cold passages, on stage doorsteps, or in desperation under the public portico on the street; and when a hundred snubs and subterfuges would culminate in the return of his manuscript, ragged but unread; I know, and I knew then, that the wreck who would dodge me in Fleet Street, or cut me in the Strand, had taken to his glass more seriously and more steadily than a man should. But I am not sure that it matters much—*much*, you understand me—when that man's heart is broken.

"The last words I was ever to exchange with my poor old friend ring in my head to this day, whenever I think of him; and I can repeat them every one. It was years after our intimacy had ceased, and when I only knew that he had degenerated into a Fleet Street loafer of the most dilapidated type, that I caught sight of him one day outside a theatre. It was the theatre which was for some years a gold-mine to one Morton Morrison, of whom you may never have heard; but he was a public pet in his day, and his day was just then at its high noon. Well, there stood Pharazyn, with his hands in his pockets and a cutty-pipe sticking out between his ragged beard and moustache, and his shoulders against the pit door, so that for once he could not escape me. But he wouldn't take a hand out of his pocket to shake mine; and when I asked him how he was, without thinking, he laughed in my face, and it made me feel cruel. He was dreadfully emaciated and almost in rags. And as I wondered what I ought to do, and what to say next, he gave a cough, and spat upon the pavement, and I could see the blood.

"I don't know what you would have done for him, but for all I knew what had brought him to this, I could think of nothing but a drink. It was mid-winter, and I tell you the man was in rags. I felt that if I could get him to a bar he might eat something, too, and that I should lay such a hold of him this time as I need never again let go. Judge of my surprise when he flatly refused to come with me even for a drink.

"'Can't you see?' he said in his hollow voice. 'There'll be a crowd here directly, and I want the best seat in the pit—the best in the house. I've been going dry for it these two days, and I'm going dry till I've seen the piece. No, I've been here an hour already, and I'm still the first; but I mightn't be when I came back, and I'm not going to risk it, thanks all the same.'

"By this I had remembered that Morton Morrison was to re-open that night with a new piece. Indeed, I ought not to have forgotten that, seeing that I had my order about me somewhere, and it meant a column from my pen between twelve and one in the morning. But this sudden sorry meeting had put all other thoughts out of my head.

"'My dear fellow,' I said, with a sort of laugh, 'are you a first-nighter, too?'

"'Only at this theatre.'

"He looked me queerly in the face.

"'You admire Morrison as much as all that?'

"'I love him!'

"I suppose my eyes thawed him, though God knows how hard I was trying not to hurt him with pitying looks. At all events he began to explain himself of his own accord, in one bitter, swift, impetuous outburst.

"'Look here,' he said, with his hoarse voice lowered: 'I hoped never to see your face again. I hoped you'd never see mine. But now you are here, don't go this minute, and I'll tell you why I think so much of Morton Morrison. I don't know him, mind you—he doesn't know me from Adam—but once long ago I had something to do with him. And God bless him, but damn every other manager in London, for he was the only one of the lot to give me a civil hearing and a kind word!'

"I knew what he was talking about, and he knew that I knew, for we had understood one another in the old days.

"'I took it to him last of all,' he went on, wiping his damp lips with his hand. 'When I began hawking it about he was an unknown man; when his turn came he was here. He let me read it to him. Then he asked me to leave it with him for a week; and when I went back to him, he said what they'd all said—that it would never act. But Morton Morrison said it nicely. And when he saw how it cut me up into little bits, he got me to tell him all about everything; and then he persuaded me to burn the play, instead of ruining my life for it; and I burnt it in his dressing-room fire, but the ruin was too far gone to mend. I wrote that thing with my heart's blood—old man, you know I did! And none of them would think of it—my God! But Morrison

- 44 -

was good about it—he's a good soul—and that's why you'll see me at every first night of his until the drink does me.'

"I had not followed him quite to the end. One thing had amazed me too much.

"'You burnt your play,' I could only murmur, 'when it would have turned into such a novel! Surely you have some draft of it still?'

"'I burnt the lot when I got home,' says Pharazyn, 'and before long I shall join 'em and burn too.'

"I had nothing to answer to that, and was, besides, tenacious of my point. 'I don't think much of the kindness that makes one man persuade another to burn his work and throw up the sponge,' I said, with a good deal of indignation, for I did feel wroth with that fellow Morrison—a bread-and-butter drawing-room actor whose very vogue used to irritate me.

"'Then what do you think of this?' asked Pharazyn, as he dipped a hand within his shabby coat, and cautiously unclenched it under my nose.

"'It's a five-pound note.'

"'I know; but wasn't *that* kind, then?'

"'So Morrison gave you this!' I said.

"Two or three persons had stopped to join us at the pit door, and Pharazyn hastily put the note back in his pocket. As he did so, his dreadfully shabby condition gave my heart a fresh cut.

"'Are you never going to spend that?' I asked in a whisper; and in a whisper he answered, 'Never. It's all my play has brought me—all. It was given me as a charity, but I took it as my earnings—my earnings for all the work and waiting, and flesh and blood and self-respect, that one thing cost me. Spend it? Not I. It will bury me as decently as I deserve.'

"We could converse no more. And the presence of other people prevented me from giving him my overcoat, though I spoke of it into his ear, begging and imploring him to come away and take it while there was still time for him to slip back and get a seat in the front row. But he would not hear of it, and the way he refused reminded me of his old stubborn independence; all I got was a promise that he would have a bite with me after the performance. And so I left him in the frosty dusk, ill-clad and unkempt, with the new-lit lamp over the pit door shining down upon the haggard mask that had once been the eager, memorable face of my cleverest friend.

"I saw him next the moment I entered the theatre that evening, and I nodded my head to him, which he rebuked with the slightest shake of his own. So I looked no more at him before the play began, comprehending that he desired me not to do so. The temptation, however, was too strong to go on resisting, for while Pharazyn was in the very centre of the front row in the pit, I was at one end of the last row of the stalls; and I was very anxious about him, wanting to make sure that he was there and not going to escape me again, and nervous at having him out of my sight for five minutes together.

"Thus I know more about the gradual change which came over Pharazyn's poor face, as scene followed scene, than of the developments and merits of those scenes themselves. My mind was in any case running more on my lost friend than on the piece; but it was not till near the end of the first act that the growing oddity of his look first struck me.

"His eyebrows were raised; it was a look of incredulity chiefly; yet I could see nothing improbable in the play as far as it had gone. I was but lightly attending, for my own purposes, as you youngsters skim your betters for review; but thus far the situation struck me as at once feasible and promising. Also it all seemed somehow familiar to me; I could not say just where or why, for watching Pharazyn's face. And it was his face that told me at last, in the second act. By God, it was his own play!

"It was Pharazyn's play, superficially altered all through, nowhere substantially; but the only play for me, when I knew that, was being acted in the front row of the pit, and not on the stage, to which I had turned the side of my head. I watched my old friend's face writhe and work until it stiffened in a savage calm; and watching, I thought of the 'first night' he had pictured jovially in the old days, when the bare idea of the piece was bursting his soul; and thinking, I wondered whether it could add a drop to his bitterness to remember that too.

"Yet, through all my thoughts, I was listening, intently enough now. And in the third act I heard the very words my friend had written: they had not meddled with his lines in the great scene which had moved us both to tears long ago in my rooms. And this I swear to, whether you believe it or no— that at the crisis of that scene, which was just as Pharazyn made it, the quiet ferocity transfiguring his face died suddenly away, and I saw it shining as once before with the sweetest tears our eyes can shed—the tears of an artist over his own work.

"And when the act was over he sat with his head on his hand for some minutes, drinking in the applause, as I well knew; then he left his seat and squeezed out on my side of the house, and I made sure he was coming to speak to me over the barrier, and got up to speak to him; but he would not see me, but stood against the barrier with a face as white and set as chiselled marble.

"What followed on the first fall of the curtain I can tell you as quickly as it happened. Louder call for an author I never heard, and I turned my eyes to the stage in my intense curiosity to see who would come forward; for the piece had been brought out anonymously; and I divined that Morrison himself was about to father it. And so he did: but as the lie passed his lips, and in the interval before the applause—the breathless interval between flash and peal—the lie was given him in a roar of fury from my left: there was a thud at my side, and Pharazyn was over the barrier and bolting down the gangway towards the stage. I think he was near making a leap for the footlights and confronting Morrison on his own boards; but the orchestra came between, and the fiddlers rose in their places. Then he turned wildly to us pressmen, and I will say he had our ear, if not that of the whole house besides, for the few words he was allowed to utter.

"'Gentlemen!' he cried at the top of his voice—'Gentlemen, I'm one of you! I'm a writing man like yourselves, and I wrote this play that you've seen. That man never wrote it at all—I wrote it myself! That man has only altered it. I read it to him two years ago—two years ago, gentlemen! He kept it for a week, and then got me to burn it as rubbish—when he had made a copy of it! And he gave me this, gentlemen—this—this—that I give him back!'

"It was a matter of only a few seconds, but not till my own last hour shall I forget Morrison's painted face on the stage, or that sweating white one beneath the boxes; or the fluttering from Pharazyn's poor fingers of the five-pound note he had treasured for two years; or the hush all over the house until the first hand was laid upon his dirty collar.

"'What!' he screamed, 'do none of you believe me? Will none of you stand by me—isn't there a man—not one man——'

"And they threw him out with my name on his lips. And I followed, and floored a brute who was handling him roughly. And nothing happened to me—because of what happened to Pharazyn."

The dear old boy sat silent, his grey head on his hand. Presently he went on, more to himself than to me: "What could I do? What proof had I? He had burnt them every one. And as long as the public would stand him, Morrison kept his good name at least. And that play was his great success!"

I ventured gently to inquire what had happened to Pharazyn.

"He died in my arms," my old friend cried, throwing up his head with an oath and a tear. "He died in a few minutes outside the theatre. I could hear them clapping after he was dead—clapping his piece."

THE WIDOW OF PIPER'S POINT

On the green shores of Sydney harbour, in a garden bounded by the beach, there sat long ago a wizened, elderly gentleman and a middle-aged, sweet-faced woman in widow's weeds. It was a glaring afternoon in early summer, but a bank of ferns protected the couple from the sun, the blue waters of Port Jackson frothed coolly upon the ribbon of golden sand at their feet, and the gentleman at all events was suitably attired. He wore a pair of nankeen trousers, fitting very close and strapped under the instep, with a surtout of the same material. A very tall, very narrow-brimmed hat rested on the ground between his chair and that of the lady; and his card, still lying in her lap, proclaimed a first visit on the part of Major Thomas Blacker, late of the Royal Artillery, but now relegated to Rose Bay, New South Wales.

Mrs. Astley was, in fact, a new and interesting arrival in the settlement, who, having found the cottage to the south-east of Point Piper untenanted when she landed, had taken it within a week of that time, as if to eschew her new world as she had fled the old. Her nearest neighbour was the major himself, who lived on the opposite shore of Rose Bay, a mile away by land and half that distance by water. He had not been five minutes in the widow's garden when he pointed across the bay with his cane, and called her attention to a sunlit window blazing among the trees.

"That's my place, madam," said the major in an impressive voice. "You can't see it properly for the scrub; but that's where you'll find me when you require my services. I'm afraid you'll have trouble with your convict servants; if you don't you'll be different from everybody else; when you do, you come to me."

The widow bowed and smiled, and asked her visitor whether it was long since he had been in England. It was seven years: there had been sad changes in the time. George the Fourth was gone, and poor dear Edmund Kean; the stalls would never look upon his like again. No, the theatre in Sydney was of the poorest description; madam must not dream of going there, at least not without the major's protection. Madam had entertained no such dream; she was merely making talk. A green-backed, paper-covered book lay on her lap with the major's card; she handed him the book, and asked him whether he had heard of it. He had not, nor of the author either. "Posthumous Papers," eh? Melancholy sound about it: was it worth reading?

"Worth reading?" said Mrs. Astley, with a pardonable smile. "Well, it is considered so in England; but I doubt whether anybody ever found any book so well worth reading as I have found this: it has made me forget a great sorrow when nothing else could—forget it by the hour together! It is still appearing in monthly parts. I am going to have the remaining numbers sent out to me, and I can lend you the early ones."

"Ah, very kind of you, I'm sure," remarked the major; but he was thinking of something else. "I can't imagine what can have brought you to such a God-forsaken spot as this!" he cried out.

"Because it *is* forsaken," murmured the widow.

"But alone!"

"I wish to be alone."

The major picked up his hat.

"Madam," said he, "I would not for the world prolong an unwelcome intrusion; yet if you knew this settlement as I know it you would understand the anxiety of an old stager like myself to render you all the assistance, and I may say the protection, in my power. It may seem officious to you now, but you will understand it, my dear madam, when you've been out here as long as I have." And with that the major held out his hand; but Mrs. Astley laid hers upon his arm.

"I understand it already," she replied, sweetly; "it is you who misunderstand me. I do appreciate your kindness in coming to see me like this; you will know it, too, the first difficulty I am in; for I shall not hesitate to take you at your generous word. And I shall always be glad to receive you, sir, when you will do me the honour of calling. Only I have suffered deeply. I am here to avoid society, not to seek it, and—but surely, Major Blacker, you can sympathise with me there?"

"I can indeed," cried the honest major. "It was the death of my own dear wife that drove *me* to New South Wales."

The fact, however (and it was one), was scarcely stated with the pathos it deserved; the gallant speaker being occupied, indeed, in noting the few lines and the many beauties of the comely face so compassionately raised to his.

"Then our case is the same, and we must be friends," said the widow very gently, as she rose. And she accompanied her visitor to the gate, keeping him waiting, however, on the way, while she found the early numbers of her book.

"Read them," she said, "and you will come for more. Oh, how I envy you having to begin at the very beginning, and not knowing one word of what is to come! I shall hear you laughing across the bay! Oh, yes, I will come and see your house one day; but I can come no further as I am, and here is the gate."

"One moment, ma'am," said the major, glancing at a man who was at work in the front garden, and lowering his voice. "A convict?"

"Yes."

"A gentleman convict, as they say, by the cut of him," muttered the major; "and that's the very worst sort. Look you, madam, if that fellow gives you the slightest trouble, you let me know."

"What could you do?"

"Get him fifty lashes!" replied the major vindictively. "I should have mentioned that I happen to be a magistrate of the colony. You may bring your man before me in my own house any day you like, and for the first piece of impudence he shall have his fifty. I also happen to possess some private influence with the Governor. I need hardly say that it would be my privilege to use it in your interest, could you but show me the way."

"You have influence with the Governor?" cried the widow, with an animation which she had not hitherto displayed, and which vastly enhanced her charms. "Then get my poor gardener, not fifty lashes, but his ticket-of-leave!"

The other gazed upon her with kindling admiration, and a pleasant, smiling tolerance.

"A philanthropist!" said he. "An enthusiast in philanthropy! Only wait, my dear lady, until you've been out here a little longer. Why, I shall have the fellow before me in a week!"

And taking off his hat as he spoke, the major jerked his bald head in the direction of the convict gardener, and departed chuckling; but turned more thoughtful on the way, and reached home walking slowly, his yellow face ploughed with thought. Major Blacker was sixty years of age, but he never considered himself an old man, and now of a sudden he felt full ten years younger. He consulted his glass when he got in; the climate had dried him up a little; but there were black hairs in his whiskers yet, and a youthful glitter in his mirrored eyes which he hoped had not been wanting in the late interview. Major Blacker had lived; and now the desire was come to him to live a little more. Turning from the mirror to his bedroom window he beheld the smoke of the widow's cottage making a grey lane through the sunset; in between and down below the fretted floor of the bay was rosy indeed from shore to shore; overhead an incredible blue was fast changing to richest purple. And to such accompaniments of the eye, and in blood as cold as you please, the major's mind was made up.

Two days later—in a community which counted three men to the woman, there was no time to be lost—in two days, therefore, Major Blacker presented himself once more at the widow's cottage. He had devoured his *Pickwick* to the last line of the second number, and the book armed him both with a topic of familiar conversation and an excuse for a second visit so precipitate. He needed numbers three and four; but the widow was from home; the assigned servant had taken her out in a boat.

The assigned servant! the gardener! in that harbour full of sharks! The major strode through the cottage, was shown the boat rounding Shark Island homeward bound, and elected to await the lady's landing in her own garden. He must speak seriously to Mrs. Astley. It was bad enough for an unprotected woman to live alone in that lonely place with a convict man-servant and a maid who was doubtless a convict also. But to trust herself upon the water with the male criminal and none beside! It was worse than madness. The poor lady was in need of a friend to warn her of her danger, and she should find that friend in Thomas Blacker.

The major stood twirling his moustaches by the water's edge until the boat's keel slid into the sand. His eye was on the convict, a tall, bearded, round-shouldered man, who hung his head (as well he might, thought the major) before that ferocious orb. It was the visitor who helped Mrs. Astley to alight on dry land, and there and then broke out, without a word of apology for his presence in her garden. Did she know what she was doing—trusting herself in that cockleshell with a transported ruffian—a desperado who would murder her in a minute if it seemed worth his while? Had no one told her the harbour was full of sharks? But the land sharks in Sydney itself, the felons and malefactors stalking at large there in the light of day, were as bad and worse; yet she could trust herself willingly to one of these!

Mrs. Astley had changed colour at his words.

"Hush!" she cried at last. "He will hear you."

"He!" exclaimed the martinet. "What do I care what *he* hears? Let him listen and take heed."

"But *I* care," insisted the lady in an imploring voice. "I take an interest in the poor fellow. I am sorry for him. He has been telling me all about his trouble."

"Trouble!" sneered the major. "That's what they all call it. What's his name?"

"Whybrow."

"Not Whybrow the forger?"

"Yes."

"Then all I can say, my dear lady," cried the major in his most pompous manner, "is that I sincerely hope you have brought no plate or valuables to this accursed country; if you have I beg of you to let me take them to my bank to-morrow. Whybrow might hesitate to cut your throat—I doubt if he has the pluck for one thing—but he'll rob you as sure as you stand there. I remember his case very well. A more accomplished villain has never been transported. He'd rob a church, so you may be quite sure he'll rob you; it's only a question of time and opportunity."

Mrs. Astley turned on her heel, took a few quick steps towards the house, turned again and rejoined her neighbour.

"Has he ever got into trouble out here?" she demanded. "Has he once been up before you or any one of your brother magistrates? Is there anything at all against him but the single offence for which he was transported?"

"Not that I know of," admitted the other with a shrug; "but he's a clever man, he would naturally behave pretty well."

"So well that you didn't even know he was in the settlement; yet you are ready, for that one crime in the past, to credit him with any villainy present or to come! Oh, can you wonder that men grow worse out here, if that is all you expect of them? If you treat your convicts like dogs, whip them like dogs, and never credit them with a single remnant of their native manhood, how can you expect ever to make them into the men they were? Yet what is this country for, if not to give the wicked and the weak another chance, a fresh start? Oh, I have no patience with your view, sir, that once a villain is always one; I have heard it on all sides of me since I landed; but I tell you it is abominable—hateful—inhuman—immoral!"

Major Blacker bowed his head. His eyes could not conceal their admiration; the fire in hers was a revelation to him; he had sought a woman and found a queen, and the falseness (to his mind) of her premiss took not a whit from his delight.

"Madam," said he, pointing with his cane to the subject of this argument, who had drawn up the boat and was carrying in the oars; "madam, I am only sorry for one thing. I am only sorry I am not yonder gardener, with you for my champion and defender! I withdraw every word I have said. Assigned to you, I can well believe that the greatest rogue in the settlement would soon become an honest man!"

"It depends so entirely on us," cried the widow, never heeding the compliments in her enthusiasm. "Oh, I think we have so much to answer for! In his last place he was treated horribly; it was up the country; no, I must not mention names, only I know from Whybrow that the chain-gang was rest and peace after what he had gone through at that man's hands. It was from a chain-gang he came to me. He has been nearly three years in the colony. He was transported for seven. Oh, don't you think it would be possible to get him his ticket this summer?"

The major felt a warm hand upon his arm; the major saw eyes of liquid blue, lit with enthusiasm, and gazing appealingly into his own. They had reached the cottage, and were standing in a tiny morning-room filled with flowers and heavy with their scent. The major felt younger than ever.

"I could try," he said, "but I fear it wouldn't be much good. Four years' servitude is the limit. I'm afraid we shouldn't have much chance."

"Try!" said the widow. "It would be an act of humanity, and one for which I should feel personally grateful all my life."

The major tried, and won the gratitude without achieving the result desired. Perhaps he did not try quite so hard as he pretended, and perhaps in time the widow detected in him a lukewarmness for the cause upon which she had set her unreasonable heart; at all events the major failed to make the quick advance he had counted upon in Mrs. Astley's affections. At the end of the summer their friendship was still nothing more, and the convict gardener still a convict gardener. As neighbours, the pair would read together the *Pickwick* numbers as they came and play an occasional game of cribbage in the major's verandah; but as sure as that veteran uttered a sentimental word touching his lonely condition or hers (and the one involved the other), so surely would the widow rise and beg him to escort her home. Nor did the view from the Old Point Piper Road soften her at all with its sparkling moonlit brilliance. Yet it was here, early in the following summer, that the gallant old fellow, after an extra half-bottle with his dinner, at last declared himself.

Mrs. Astley heard him with an expressionless face turned towards the harbour; but ere he finished, the moonlight that strewed those waters with shimmering gems had found two also in her eyes.

"I cannot," she cried. "I loved my husband—I love him still—I shall never marry again!"

"But so did I love my sainted wife," protested the major; "yet I would marry to-morrow. I consider it no disrespect to the dead; on the contrary, it is the highest compliment we can pay them, as showing so happy an experience of wedlock that we would fain repeat it. Not that I have thought so always," he added hastily, to quell a look which made him uncomfortable.

"I don't believe you think so now," replied the candid widow. "You not only mean less than you say; you feel less; and must forgive me, for you may not know it yourself, but a woman is never deceived. Think it over and you will agree with me; but never, never let us speak of this again. It hurts me to hurt you—and I like you so much as a friend!"

As for Thomas Blacker, the first plunge had completely sobered him, and he bitterly repented that indiscretion of the table which had led him into a declaration as premature as it had been also unpremeditated. As a soldier, however, he took no kindlier to retreat for the mere fact of deploring his advance; retreat, indeed, was out of the question: and the major's further protestations were pitched in a key calculated to acquit him of a charge which rankled, being true.

"Your answer I accept, and can bear," he retorted with dignity, "but not your misjudgment of my feelings. That would be cruel—if you were capable of cruelty. Permit me at least to say that it shows an ignorance of my real nature which cuts me to the quick. I have expressed myself but poorly if you can still doubt my readiness to devote my life to you—ay, or to lay it down if need be for your sake! There is nothing I would not do for you. The lightest service I should esteem my privilege."

The widow laughed, but not unkindly; on the contrary, her hand slid through the major's arm with her words, as if to sheath their edge.

"There was one thing you once promised to do for me," she said. "It is not done yet!"

"I know what you mean," he groaned with an inward oath. "Your assigned gardener!"

"Exactly."

"I tried my best."

"Could you not try again?"

"If I did," said the major hoarsely, "would it make any difference to the answer you would give me if I said again what I have said to-night? I tell you candidly I begin to feel jealous of that convict. I shall be glad to see his back."

The woman gave a little nervous laugh, but no answer.

"Would it make any difference?" he repeated.

"I cannot bargain like that," sighed the widow, turning away.

"And you are right!" exclaimed the other, hotly flushing. "I unsay that; I'm ashamed of it. But I'll get that ticket-of-leave this summer, or I'll never look you in the face again!"

And this time Thomas Blacker went to work in earnest; but then a year had passed since his former half-hearted attempt of foregone futility; and the forlorn hope of that season was the easy goal of this. The major, without doubt, stood well at Government House; he was secretly engaged upon plans for the fortifications of the harbour, and had the ear of his Excellency in magisterial matters as well. What he had mentioned only tentatively and not altogether seriously the year before, he now urged as a peculiarly deserving case. And in no more than a day or two he had the pleasure of calling at the cottage, with a paper for the widow to sign, and of meeting the gardener on the path as he was coming away.

"I suppose you know what I have here, my man?" cried the major, tapping a breast inflated with conscious benevolence.

"The mistress has mentioned it," replied the man, trembling in an instant. "I am deeply grateful, sir, to you. I little thought to get it yet."

"Nor have you, sir, nor have you," said the major briskly. "Your ticket's no ticket till it's signed by the Governor and safe in your hands. However," he added, with a touch of the self-importance he enjoyed, "I have promised your mistress to use my influence in your behalf, so by the end of the week you may very possibly hear from me again."

And as if to finish the thing off with a flourish Thomas Blacker was finally even better than his word, for, as far from the end of the week as the Wednesday evening, he dined in Sydney and rode out by moonlight and the Point Piper Road with Whybrow's ticket signed and sealed in his pocket. Once more the major had dined well, but this time not unwisely; yet his heart was troubled with a trouble which had never entered his calculations hitherto. His brother was dead; his brother's estates were now his own. The incoming mail had brought the news, and with it a round of applause and congratulations from connections and friends who for years had ignored his existence. The major was in a private quandary of the spirit; he was quite unable to make up his mind. Should he go home a married man, or should he see his time-serving friends to the deuce and never go home at all? The tropic moon and the heavenly harbour inclined him to the latter, certain phrases in his home-letters to the former course; but what about his wife? She was qualified to adorn any society in which the major had ever moved, but—there were buts. The major was gallant enough to try to ignore them, but there they were. At home he was not sure that he should want to be married at all; here it was a different thing; and here, no doubt, he would end his days after all. There were worse places. These moonlight nights made the place a paradise of soft airs and rustling leaves, and miles and miles of a jewelled carpet beneath the white-starred ceiling of the Southern sky. Yes, it was a spot to live and die in, and be thankful; and yes!

he would marry the widow, if the widow would marry him. And after the other night——

The major had reached the cottage gate. Here he dismounted, tethering his horse within. There were voices and lights, both low, in the cottage; the French windows were wide open to the night; and an ignoble instinct, begotten of a swift suspicion that was more truly an inspiration, caused the major to advance upon the grass. So he crept nearer—nearer yet—within earshot. And the first words he heard confirmed him in his deceit. By heaven! there should be trick for trick!

"Darling," said the widow's voice—the sweet voice that had beguiled him—"it will be the end of the week to-morrow—well, then, next day; and after that we will hide it no more. Let us brazen it out! I am always ready; and you, you will have the right to take care of me as you should: you will have your ticket-of-leave."

"Never!" muttered the major between his teeth, and he crushed up the paper he held ready in his hand. He forgot his doubts upon the moonlit road. The injured man was all the man now. He crept still nearer and saw that for which he was now so fully prepared: the widow reposing in the convict's arms.

"There's only one thing that troubles me," the man was saying (though his twitching, restless face was an eternal sea of trouble and remorse), "and that is your poor old major. He has turned up trumps" ("I'm damned if he has," muttered the major behind the leaves), "and it does seem a shame. I fear the other night you must have led him on."

"I did," replied the woman, with a groan for which she received no credit. "I did—I could not help it. It grieves me to think of it; I am so ashamed; but, darling, it was for you!"

"Was it indeed?" cried the major, striding into the room with sounding heels and jingling spurs; and he stood there twirling his moustache. The woman was first upon her feet. The man's face sank into his hands.

"It was," she repeated boldly. "And oh, sir, even you will forgive me when I tell you all!"

"Naturally," sneered the other—"if I stopped to listen. But explanations I imagine would be somewhat superfluous after this. Here, you may have it," he added, opening his hand and letting the crumpled ticket drop with an air of ineffable contempt. "I won't condescend to put it back in my pocket, as you deserve; take it—and marry the man, for God's sake, at the nearest church!"

The woman laid a tender hand upon the bowed and bended head at which Thomas Blacker glanced in righteous scorn.

"Marry him I cannot," said she. "We have been married these fifteen years."

AFTER THE FACT

I

It is my good fortune to cherish a particularly vivid recollection of the town of Geelong. Others may have found the place so dull as to justify an echo of the cheap local sneer at its expense; to me those sloping parallels of low houses have still a common terminus in the bluest of all Australian waters; and I people the streets, whose very names I have forgotten, with faces of extraordinary kindness, imperishable while memory holds her seat. Even had it bored me, I for one should have good reason to love Geelong. It was my lot, however, not only to happen upon the town in a week of unique excitement, but, thanks to one of those chance meetings which are the veriest commonplace of outlandish travel, to have a finger in the pother. I arrived by the boat on a Monday afternoon, to find the streets crowded and peace disturbed by a sudden run on one of the banks. On the Wednesday, another bank, which had notoriously received much of the money withdrawn from the Barwon Banking Company, Limited, was in its turn the victim of a still uglier fate: the Geelong branch of the Intercolonial was entered in broad daylight by a man masked and armed to the beard, who stayed some ten minutes, and then walked into thin air with no less a sum than nineteen thousand and odd pounds in notes and gold.

I was playing lawn-tennis with my then new friends when we heard the news; and it stopped our game. The bank manager's wife, a friend of my friends, arrived with her daughter: the one incoherent, the other dumb, with horror and dismay. And I heard at first-hand a few broken, hysterical words from the white lips of the elderly lady, and noted the tearless trouble in the wide blue eyes of the girl, before it struck me to retire. The family had been at luncheon in the private part of the bank, and knew nothing of the affair until the junior clerk broke in upon them like a lunatic at large. He, too, had gone out for his lunch, and returned to find teller and cashier alike insensible, and the safe rifled. That was all I stayed to gather, save that the unhappy lady was agitated by a side issue far worse to her than the bank's loss. There had been no bloodshed. The revolver kept beneath the counter had been used, but used in vain. It was not loaded. Her husband would be blamed, nay, discharged to a certainty in his old age. And I, too, walked down the street more absorbed in the picture of an elderly couple brought to ruin, and a blue-eyed girl gone for a governess, than in the immediate catastrophe.

I found my way to the Intercolonial Bank; there was no need to ask it. A crowd clamoured at the doors, but these were shut for the day. And I learned no more than I already knew, save that the robber wore a black beard, and was declared by some to be a second Ned Kelly from the Strathbogie Ranges. Nor did I acquire more real information the rest of that day; nor hope for any when late at night I thought I recognised an old schoolfellow in the street.

"Deedes *major!*" I cried without pausing to make certain; but I was certain enough when my man turned and favoured me with the stare of studied insolence which had made our house-master's life a burden to him some ten years before that night. Among a thousand, although the dark eyes were sunken and devil-may-care, the full lips hidden by a moustache with grey hairs in it, and the pale face prematurely lined, I could have sworn to Deedes *major* then.

"Don't know you from Adam," said he. "What do you want?"

"We were at school together," I explained. "I was your fag when you were captain of footer. To think of meeting you here!"

"Do tell me your name," he said wearily; and at that moment I recollected (what had quite escaped my memory) his ultimate expulsion; and I stood confounded by my maladroitness.

"Bower," said I, abashed.

"The Beetle!" cried Deedes, not unkindly; a moment later he was shaking my hand and smiling on my confusion. "Hang school!" said he. "Where are you staying?"

"Well," said I, "I'm supposed to be staying with some people I brought a letter of introduction to; but they hadn't a room for me, and insisted on getting me one outside; so that's where I am."

"What's their name?" said Deedes; when I told him, he nodded, but made no further comment, beyond inviting himself to my room for a chat. The proposal delighted me; indeed it caused me a positive thrill, which I can only attribute to an insensible return of the small boy's proper attitude towards a distinguished senior. We were twenty-eight and twenty-four now, instead of eighteen and fourteen; yet, as we walked, only one of us was a man, and I was once more his fag. I felt quite proud when he accepted a cigarette from my case, prouder yet when he took my arm. The feeling stuck to me till we reached my room, when it suddenly collapsed. Deedes had asked me what I was doing. I had told him of my illness and my voyage, and had countered with his own question. He laughed contemptuously, sitting on the edge of my bed.

"Clerk in a bank!" said he.

"Not the Intercolonial?" I cried.

"That's it," he answered, nodding.

"Then you were there to-day! This *is* luck; I've been so awfully keen to know exactly what happened."

"I was not there," replied Deedes. "I was having my lunch. I can only tell you what I saw when I got back. There was our cashier sprawled across the counter, and the teller in a heap behind it—both knocked on the head. And there was the empty safe, wide open, with the sun shining into it like a bull's-eye lantern. No, I only wish I *had* been there: it's such a chance as I shall never get again."

"You'd have shown fight?" said I, gazing at his long athletic limbs, and appreciating the force of his wish as I perceived in what threadbare rags they were imprisoned. "Yes, you'd have stood up to the chap, I know; I can see you doing it!"

"There would have been nothing wonderful in that," was his reply. "I should have had everything to gain and nothing to lose."

"Not your life?"

"It's less than nothing."

"Nonsense, Deedes," said I, although or because I could see that it was not. "You don't expect me to believe that!"

"I don't care what you believe, and it's not the point," he answered. "Give me another cigarette, Beetle; you were asking about the robbery; if you don't mind, we'll confine ourselves to that. I'm afraid old I'Anson will get the sack; he's the manager, and responsible for the bank revolver being loaded. He swears it was; we all thought it was; but nobody had looked at it for weeks, and you see it wasn't. Yes, that's a rule in all banks in this country where sticking them up is a public industry. The yarn about Ned Kelly's son? Don't you believe it; nobody ever heard of him before. No, if you ask me, we must look a little nearer home for the man who stuck up our bank this afternoon."

"Nearer home!" said I. "Then you think it was somebody who knew about the run upon the Barwon Banking Company and the payments into the Intercolonial?"

"Obviously; somebody who knew all about it, and perhaps paid in a big lump himself. That would have been a gorgeous blind!" cried Deedes, kindling suddenly. "Beetle, old chap, I wish I'd thought of it myself—only it would have meant boning the capital too! I strongly suspect some of these respectable Geelongese and Barwonners of being at the bottom of the whole thing, though; they're *so* respectable, Beetle, there's bound to be villains among 'em. By Jove!" he added, getting to his feet with a sinister light in his handsome, dissipated countenance, "I'll go for the reward when they put it up! Four figures it can't fall short of; that would be better than junior clerking for eighty pounds a year!" And he walked up and down my room laughing softly to himself.

"I'll join you," cried I. "I'll go in for love, or honour and glory, and you shall pocket the £ s. d."

"Rot!" said he curtly, yet almost with the word he had me by the shoulders, and was smiling queerly in my face. "Why not join me in the other thing?" he exclaimed. "You were well enough plucked at school!"

"But what other thing?" said I.

"Doing the trick," he cried; "not finding out who did it!"

"Deedes," said I, "what the devil do you mean?"

"Mean? What I say, my dear Beetle—every word of it! What's the use of being honest? Look at me. Look at my shirt-cuffs, that I've got to trim every morning like my nails; look at my trousers, as I saw you looking at 'em just now. Those bags at the knees are honesty; and honesty's rapidly wearing them through on an office stool. I'm as poor as a rat in a drain: it's all honesty, and I've had about enough of it. Think of the fellow who walked off with his fortune this morning, and then think of me. Wouldn't you like to be in his shoes? No? My stars, you don't know what it is to live, Beetle; honest idiots like us never do. But I'm going to turn it up. If one can play at that game, two can; why not three? Come on, Beetle; make a third, and we'll rob another bank to-morrow!"

"You're joking," said I, and this time I returned his smile. "Still, if I was going in for that sort of thing, Deedes, I don't know who I'd rather have on my side than you."

His smile went out like a light.

"Will you go in for it?" he cried. "I'm joking far less than you think. My life's a sordid failure. I'm sick of it and ready for a fling. Will you come in?"

"No," I said. "I won't."

And we looked each other steadily in the eyes, until he led me back to laughter with as much ease as he had lengthened my face.

"All right, old Beetle!" said he. "I won't chaff any more—not that it was all chaff by any means. I sometimes feel like that, and so would you in my place. Bunked from school! In disgrace at home! Sent out here to be got rid of, sent to blazes in cold blood! The things I've done for a living during these ten years—this is the most respectable, I can tell you that. It's the respectability drives me mad."

His bitter voice, the lines upon his face, his grey hairs at twenty-eight (they were not confined to his moustache), all appealed to me with equal and irresistible force; my hand went out to him, and with it my heart.

"I am so sorry, Deedes," said I nervously. "If a fiver or two—yes, you must let me! For the sake of the old school!"

He shook his head, and the blood rushed to mine. I burst into apologies, but he cut me short.

"That's all right, Beetle. It was well meant, and you're a good chap. We'll foregather to-morrow, if this enviable stroke leaves us a spare moment in the bank. Meanwhile good-night, and thanks all the same."

And he crept down the stairs at my request; for I was not in the position of an ordinary lodger; and having followed and closed the door noiselessly behind him, I returned as stealthily to my room. I did not wish my hospitable friends to know that I had used lodgings, placed at my disposal as their guest, as though I had engaged them on my own account. Theoretically I was under their roof, and had committed a breach in introducing a man at midnight and sitting up in conversation with him till all hours. Deedes, moreover, as I suspected from his manner when I mentioned them, was most probably no friend of my friends; indeed I had no clue to his reputation in the town, and should have been surprised to find it a good one. He had been a reckless boy at school; at the very least he was a reckless man. And other traits must have developed with his years; he had been expelled, for instance, for certain gallantries not criminal in themselves, but sufficiently demoralising at a public school; and, despite his clothes, I could have sworn those dark, unscrupulous eyes, and that sardonic, insolent, and yet attractive manner, had done due damage in Geelong.

For there was a fascination in the man, incommunicable by another, and my despair as I write. He was a strong, selfish character, one in whom the end permitted any means; yet there was that in him for which it is harder to find a name, which attracted while it repelled, which enforced admiration in its own despite. At school he had been immensely popular and a bad influence: at once a bugbear and an idol from the respective points of view of masters and boys. My own view was still that of the boy. I could not help it; nor could I sleep for thinking of our singular rencontre and interview. I undressed, but shirked my pillow. I smoked my pipe; but it did me no good. Finally I threw up my window, and as I did so heard a sound that interested, and another that thrilled me. The first was a whistle blowing in the distance; the second, an answering whistle, which made me jump, for it came from beneath the very window at which I stood.

I leaned out. A white helmet and a pair of white legs flashed under a lamp and were gone. My window was no impossible height from the ground, but I did not stay to measure it. With the whistles still in my ears I lowered myself from the sill, dropped into a flower-bed, and gave chase to the helmet and the legs, myself barefooted and in pyjamahs.

I saw my policeman vanish round a corner. I was after him like a deer, and even as I ran the position amused me. Chasing the police! He could not hear my naked feet; I gained on him splendidly, and had my hand on his shoulder before he knew me to exist. His face, as he stopped and turned it, feeling for his pistol, I shall remember all my life.

"All right," I cried. "I'm not the man you're after. Hurry up! I'm coming along to see the fun."

He swore in my teeth and rushed on. I followed in high excitement at his heels. All this time the first whistle was blowing through the night. We had reached the outskirts of the town, and were nearing the sound. At length, on turning a corner, we came upon another drill-trousered, pith-helmeted gentleman in the gateway of an empty house.

"That's about enough of us," said he, pocketing his whistle. "I've got a man already on the lawn at the back. The house is empty, and he's in it like a rat in a trap. But who's this you've brought along with you, mate?"

"A volunteer," said I. "You won't refuse to let me lend a hand if I get the chance?"

"You'll get your brains blown out," replied the constable who had given the alarm, a sergeant as I saw now. "You'd best go home, though I won't say but what we want all the men we can get. The town's asleep—as usual. Can you face powder?"

"I'll see," said I, laughing, for I scarcely suspected he was in earnest. "Who is it you're after? Somebody very dangerous?"

"The Intercolonial bank-robber," replied the sergeant grimly. "What do you say now?"

I said nothing at all. I know not what I had expected; but it was not this; and for the moment my own density concerned me as much as my fears.

"Oh, that's all right," said the sergeant, with an intolerable sneer. "You cut away and send a grown man along when you see one!"

My reply need not be recorded; suffice it that a moment later one of the men, who both carried firearms, had handed me his truncheon; and I was on my way to join the third constable on the lawn behind the house, while those two effected an entrance in front.

II

The third constable nearly shot me through the head at sight. The twinkle of his pistol caught my eye; I threw up my arms and declared myself a friend, not, as I believe, one second too soon. Never have I seen a man more pitiably excited than this brave fellow on the back lawn. Brave he was beyond all question; but cool he was not, and I fancy the combination must be rarer in real life than elsewhere. The man on the lawn stood over six feet in his boots, and every inch of him was shaking like a jelly. Yet if our quarry had chosen that moment to make a dash for it on this side, it would have gone hard with him, for my constable was suffering from nothing more discreditable than over-eagerness for the fray.

Would that I could say as much for myself! Already I entirely regretted my absurd proceeding, and longed with all my heart to escape. It was out of the question. I had put my hand most officiously to the plough, but there it must stay; and as it was too late to reconsider my position, so there was now no sense in investigating the hare-brained impulse upon which I had acted. Yet I turned it over in my mind, standing there with my naked feet in the cold dew, and I deplored my conscious cowardice no less than my unthinking folly. One thing is certain, had I reckoned at all, it was without the bank-robber, whom his would-be imitator had put quite out of my head. And here they had him in this house! We saw their lanterns moving from room to room on the ground-floor; and I should be sorry to say which of us shivered most (from what different causes), the third constable or myself.

I do not know how long we waited, but in a little the lanterns ceased to flit behind the panes. The men had evidently gone upstairs, and in the darkness we heard a sound as terrifying to me as it was evidently welcome to my companion. "At last!" said he, and crept up to the back door, open-armed. We had heard the stealthy drawing of bolts; but we were destined, one of us to disappointment, the other to inexpressible relief. The door opened, and it was the sergeant upon whom his subordinate would have pounced. He stood there, beckoning without a word; and so led us to a locked room next the kitchen. His mate had gone round the front way to watch the window; we were to force the door and carry the room by storm; and in it, declared the sergeant, we should find our man.

We did not; and again I breathed. The room was not only empty; the window was fastened on the inside; and an accumulation of the loose fittings of the house, evidently for sale to the incoming tenant, seemed to explain the locked door. At least I said so, and the explanation was received better than it deserved. We now proceeded, all four of us (abandoning system in our unsuccess), to search the cellar; but our man was not there, and I began to tell myself he was not in the house at all. Thus, as my companions lost their heads and rushed to the attics as one man, I found mine and elected to remain below. The room we had broken into was the one I chose to wait in; for I had explored no other, and wherever else he might be, the robber was not here. Judge then of my feelings when I heard him moving under my feet. Horror glued me where I stood, unable to call out, unable to move; my eyes fast as my feet to the floor, watching a board that moved in the dim light of a candle-end found and lit by one of the constables at our first inspection. The board moved upward; a grimy face appeared through the aperture; it was that of my old schoolfellow, Deedes *major*.

"For God's sake, Beetle, help me out of this!" he whispered.

"Deedes!" I could only murmur; and again, "Deedes!"

"Yes, yes," said he impatiently. "Think of the old school—and tell me where they are. Are they gone?"

"Only upstairs. What on earth's at the bottom of this, Deedes?" I asked him sternly.

"A mistake—a rotten mistake!" said he. "They gave chase to me shortly after I left you. I got in here, but the one chap daren't follow me alone, and I ripped up this floor and got under while he was whistling away outside. I spotted a loose board by treading on it, and that bit of luck's just saved my bacon."

"Has it? I'm not so sure," said I, walking to the door and listening. "What do they want you for?"

"Would you believe it? For sticking up the bank—when I was out at my lunch! Did you ever hear such rot?"

"I don't know; if you're an innocent man, why not behave like one? Why hide—they're coming down!" I broke off, hearing them. "Stop where you are! You can never get out in time!"

In the candle-light his face gleamed very pale between the blotches of dust and dirt; but I fancied it brightened at my involuntary solicitude.

"You will help me?" he whispered eagerly. "For the sake of the good old school," he wheedled, playing still upon the soft spot I had discovered to him earlier in the night. It was a soft spot still. I remembered him in the fifteen and the eleven; then overcame the memory, and saw him for what he was now.

"Hush!" said I from the door. "I want to listen."

"Where are they now?"

"Looking on the next landing."

"Then now's my time!"

"Not it," said I, putting my back against the door.

He rose waist-high through the floor, his dark eyes blazing, his right hand thrust within his coat; and I knew what was in the hand I could not see.

"Pot away!" I jeered. "You haven't done murder yet. You daren't do it now!"

"I dare do anything," he growled. "But you—you'll never go and give a chap away, Beetle?"

"You'll give yourself away if you don't get under that this instant. They're coming down, man! Stop where you are, and I'll see you later; try to get out of it, and I promise you you're a gone coon!"

He disappeared without a word, and I ran out to salute my comrades in the hall.

"Well," cried I, "what luck?"

"None at all," replied the sergeant angrily. "I could have sworn it was this house, but I suppose we must try the next. How we've missed him is more than I can fathom!"

A slaty sky denoted imminent dawn as we emerged from the house; the chill of dawn was in the air, and there was I in nothing but pyjamahs. One of the constables remarked upon my condition, and the sergeant (good man) made me a pathetic speech of thanks, and recommended me my bed. If they needed further assistance they could get it next door, but he was afraid his man had made a longer flight than that. And indeed when I returned to the spot, in my clothes, an hour later, there was no sign of the police in the road; and I was enabled to slip into the empty house unobserved.

I got in through an open window, broken near the hasp, by which the fugitive himself had first effected an entry. In the early morning light the place looked different and very dirty; and as I entered the room with the burst door, I thought it also very still. I tore up the loose boards, and uttered an exclamation which resounded horribly in the desolation. Deedes was gone. I poked my head below the level of the floor, but there was no sign of him underneath. As I raised myself, however, a step just sounded on the threshold, and there he stood in his socks, smiling, with a revolver in his hand.

For one instant I doubted his intention; the next, the weapon dropped into his pocket, and his smile broadened as though he had read my fear.

"No fear, Beetle," said he; "it's not for you. I couldn't be sure it was you, that was all. So you're as good as your word! I hardly expected you so soon—if at all!"

"Do you remember my word?" said I meaningly, for his coolness irritated me beyond measure. His very face and hands he had contrived to cleanse at some of the taps. He might have been in bed all night and neglected nothing but his chin and his hair. And this was the man of whom a whole colony would talk this morning, for whom a whole colony would hunt all day.

"Your word?" said Deedes. "You promised to help me."

"I didn't. I said I'd see you again. If I help you it will be on very definite terms."

"Half-profits, eh? Well, I'm agreeable, and glad you haven't forgotten our conversation of last night."

"And I'm glad," I retorted, "to see you make no more bones about your guilt. Where's the money? I want the lot."

"You're greedy, Beetle!"

"Confound you!" I cried, "do you think I want to compromise myself by being found here with you? For two pins I'll leave you to get out of this as best you can. You heard me? I want that twenty thousand pounds. I want it to pay back into the bank. Then I'll do what I can, but not until."

I saw his dark eyes blazing as they had blazed in the candle-light. He was between me and the door, and I knew that for any gain to him I never should have left that room alive. At least I believed so then; I believe it still; but at that moment his manner changed. He gave in to me, and yet maintained a coolness and a courage in his peril, a dignity in his defeat, which more than fascinated me. They made me his slave. I could have screened him all day for the pure æsthetic joy of contemplating those fearless, dare-devil eyes and hearing that cynical voice of unaffected ease. But the money I insisted on having.

"That's all very well," said he; "but I haven't got it here. I planted it."

"Tell me where."

"I can't; I could never make it plain; it's not an obvious place at all. Still I accept your terms. Bring me a change of clothes to-night—I daren't face daylight—and I give you my word you shall have the stuff to take back to the bank. I've made a bungle of it; thought of it for weeks, and bungled it after all! It was that Barwon business tempted me. I wasn't ready, but couldn't resist the big haul. All I want now is to get out of it with a whole skin. And by Jove! I see the way. You go to old I'Anson with the money, and get him to say he'll see me. Then I'll tell him it was all a practical joke—done for a bet—anything you like—and if the thing don't altogether blow over, well, I'll get off lighter than I deserve. The old chap will stand by me at all events; he's got his reasons."

I refrained from asking what they were. I fancied I knew, and hoped I did not. But Deedes demanded more than a silent consent to his plans.

"Look here: are you on, Beetle, or are you not?"

"Can I trust you?"

"I give you my word upon it; till yesterday it was the word of an honest man."

"You want a rig-out as different as possible from what you have on?"

"Yes, and some whiskers or something if you can possibly get hold of any. Your friends are great on theatricals. Ask to look at their props."

"You'll pay back every penny, and plead a practical joke?"

"My dear chap, it's my only chance. I see no other way out of it, Beetle. I'm fairly cornered; only help me to pay back before I'm caught, and at least I'll get off light."

"Very well," said I. "On those conditions I will help you. Where were you when I came in?"

"In the cellar; it's safer and also more comfortable than under the floor."

"Then I advise you to go back there, for I'm off. If I'm found here we shall be run in together."

He detained me, however, a moment more. It was to put a letter in my hand, a stout missive addressed in pencil to myself.

"You see I've been busy while you were gone," he said, in a tone quite shy for him. "Read that after your breakfast. It may make you think less ill of me. And, for the love of Heaven, deliver the enclosures!"

I undertook to do so; my interest, however, was as yet confined to the outer envelope, a clean piece of stationery, never used before.

"Upon my word," said I, "you have come prepared. No doubt you have provisions too?"

Deedes produced a packet and a flask. "Sandwiches and whisky," said he, "in case of need!"

I looked hard at him; it may have been my imagination, but for once I thought he changed colour.

"Deedes," said I, "you're a cold-blooded, calculating villain; but I confess I can't help admiring you."

"And trusting me about to-night?" he added, with some little anxiety.

"I wouldn't trust you a bit," I replied, "if it weren't to your own interest to do everything you've said you'll do. Luckily it is. There's a hue and cry for you in this town. Every hole and corner will be watched *but* the bank. You can't hope to get away; and by far your wisest plan is the one you've hit upon, to return the money and throw yourself on your manager's mercy."

"It is," he answered, with his foot upon the cellar stairs; "and you bet old I'Anson won't make it harder than necessary for me. It's a clever idea. I should never have thought of it but for you. Old man, I'm grateful; it's more than I deserve!"

And I left him with my hand aching from a grip as warm as that of any honest man; and what was stranger yet, the incredible impression of a catch in my villain's voice. Here, however, I felt I must be mistaken, but my thoughts were speedily distracted from the anomaly. I had a milkman to dodge as I made my escape from the garden of the empty house. And half-way down the road I met none other than the poor discomfited sergeant of the night.

"Been having another look at the house," said I, with the frankness that disarms suspicion.

"See anything fresh?"

"Nothing."

"You wouldn't. I don't believe the beggar was in the house two minutes. Still I thought I'd like to have a squint myself by daylight; and there'll be little damages to repair where we come in. So long, mister; you done your best; it wasn't *your* fault."

He was gone. I looked after him with my heart in my mouth. I watched him to the gate. Would he come forth alone—or alive? I saw the last of the sergeant—and fled.

III

I cannot pretend to describe my feelings of the next few hours; nor would the result be very edifying even if I succeeded in any such attempt. I trembled for the criminal's security, I quaked for the sergeant's life, but most of all I quaked and trembled for my own skin and my own peace of mind. If the sergeant captured Deedes, my flagrant complicity must inevitably leak out, and I too should have to stand my trial as accessory after the fact. If, on the other hand, Deedes murdered the sergeant, and himself escaped, the guilt of blood would gnaw my soul for ever. Thus I tossed between a material Scylla and a spiritual Charybdis, in the trough of my ignoble terrors. Every footstep in the gravel was that of some "stern-faced man" come to lead me thence "with gyves upon my wrists." Every cry from the street proclaimed the sergeant's murder in the empty house.

It was impossible to conceal my condition from my friends. With that partial and misleading candour, therefore, at which I was becoming so vile an adept, I told them of my recognition of the man whose name was now in every mouth; of our midnight conversation in my room; of the police-whistle, and my subsequent adventures in the constables' company. There I stopped; and the tale gained me a kudos, and exposed me to a fusillade of questions, which were by no means the lightest punishments of that detestable day. Again and again I felt certain I had betrayed the guilty knowledge that lay so heavy on my heart. I was quite convinced of it about eleven in the forenoon, when my host came among us perspiring from a walk.

"I've just been down to the police-station," said he, "but they haven't got him yet. The sergeant tells me——"

"Which sergeant?" I shouted.

"The man you were with last night. He has been speaking about you, Mr. Bower—speaking very highly of your behaviour last night. Nor was he the only one; it's all over the town—Girls, we have all woke up famous for having such a hero in our house!"

Famous! a hero! I thought of the names which might justly replace those words any moment. And in a sudden irresistible panic I fled the room; my flight being attributed (I afterwards discovered) to my "charming English modesty," with odious comparisons which I need not add.

Before this the young ladies of the house had been regaling me with a good many facts, and perhaps a little unintentional fiction, concerning the Geelong branch of Mr. Deedes's colonial career. It was a record highly characteristic of the Deedes who had been so popular and so infamous at school. He had won every tournament at the tennis-courts; he danced better than any man in Geelong. He had proposed to a rich Melbourne widow twice his age; had broken many hearts, including that of the blue-eyed daughter of the bank; and been seen at one dance, "well, in a state which made it impossible for us to know him any more." I had gathered from Deedes that my friends were none of his; now I was in possession of the cause; but the item affecting the Miss I'Anson whose face I had just seen the day before, and yet remembered vividly, was the item that focused my interest. I asked what sort of a girl she was. The account I received was not a little critical, yet reasonably charitable save on the part of one young lady who said nothing at all. She it was also who had said least against Deedes himself; and of this one I thought when in my panic I had broken loose from the bevy and fled to the farthest and most obscure corner of the kitchen-garden. Was she also in love with the attractive scamp? Could that Miss I'Anson with the blue eyes be in the same helpless case? Deedes had hinted at the manager's well-grounded good-will towards himself. Could there be, not a secret but a private understanding between Deedes and the daughter? He had given me a letter and spoken of enclosures which I had undertaken to deliver. Did one of them contain words of love for the sad eyes I could not forget? And if so, was I bound to keep my promise?

The letter itself I had quite forgotten in the stress of a later anxiety now happily removed. But I opened and read it among the gooseberries and the cabbages; and was myself so revolted, alike by the purport and the tone of this communication, that I have no intention of reproducing it here. It had, however, the merit of brevity; and this was the point. He had been an idiot about girls all his life. There were two at least in Geelong of whom he wished, whatever happened to him, to take a tender leave. He had written two notes, but had left them undirected, because it was not fair that I should know the names. Would I put the three-cornered note on the ledge under the eaves, at the *back* of the pavilion at the tennis-courts, and midway between the ladies' and the gentlemen's entrances? I should probably be going there that afternoon (as a matter of fact I was going), and it would take no trouble, but only a little care, to do this when nobody was near. But he would be immensely grateful to me; and still more so if I would slip the square note into the biggest book in a certain pew of the church nearest the Western Beach. He gave the number of the pew, and the exact bearings of the church, which was always open.

I pass over the thing that incensed me: his taking it so coolly for granted, before it had been granted, that I would help him in his abominable dilemma, and so connive in his felony. I had done so; but had I read this letter in his presence, I flattered myself I had shown him a stiffer front. As it was, however, these undirected billets-doux did undoubtedly recruit and renew my interest in the whole intrigue; and, promise or no promise, I should have carried out the rascal's instructions to the letter. He had counted upon the inquisitive side of my character—shall I say of human nature?—and he had counted not in vain. It was a stroke of genius on his part to leave the notes unaddressed.

I looked at my watch. We were still on the right side of noon. Going indoors for my hat, I craved permission to run to my rooms and change into flannels before lunch; and Deedes himself could not have hit upon a craftier pretext. It exempted me from escort, and thus cleared my path to the church, whither I proceeded without delay. The pew was easily found; I profaned a fat hymn-book with the square note, and crept out like the stealthy creature I was become. The church had been empty when I entered it. Coming out, however, I met a man in the porch. He was a huge, sandy-bearded, rolling walker, wearing a suit of blue serge and a straw-hat. As we passed, I saw his eye upon me; a moment later, this caused me to return upon my tracks, in order to see he did not meddle with Deedes's note. I was too late; I caught him sidling awkwardly from the pew, with the little square missive held quite openly between his fingers; and I awaited him in the porch with sensations upon which I need not dwell, beyond confessing that he appeared to me to grow six inches with every rolling stride.

"Pardon me, sir," said I, "but you've taken something that wasn't intended for you."

"How do you know that?" said he.

"It was intended for a young lady."

The big man looked down upon me through narrow eyes.

"Exactly," said he. "I am her father."

And that was all; he passed in front of me without a threatening or an insolent word, merely pocketing the note as he slouched down the churchyard path. But I, as I followed, took offence from every cubit of his stature; and could have hurled myself upon him (so depraved was I already) had I been more than half his size.

Heaven knows how I behaved at lunch! Instead of Deedes and the sergeant, the big man in the church was on my nerves. What would he do? Read the letter, of course; yet he had not even opened it, to my certain knowledge, when I lost sight of him. Would he know whom the letter was from? If so (and know he must), my illicit dealings with the wanted man would be equally plain to him; and how would this stranger deal with me? Who was he at all? and did he know in the least who *I* was, or where to lay hands on me? Should I meet him at the courts? I began to tell myself I did not care either way; that it must all come to light sooner or later now, so the sooner the better. But the man never came to the courts. As the afternoon wore on without sight or sign of him, a little confidence returned; the evening was at hand, and with it my own atonement as well as that of Deedes; and there was comfort in the thought that at the worst my false position would come to an end within the same twenty-four hours which had witnessed its assumption.

But the interim was itself charged with dramatic interests for me personally. In the first place there was the three-cornered note. Impelled by that strongest of all motives, curiosity, and thus undeterred by the fiasco of the first note, I put the second where I had been told to put it, and that before I had been five minutes on the ground. Then I played a couple of setts; but my play was even worse than usual; for I had one eye all the time upon the gate, and it would follow each new arrival to the pavilion, and seek a blush on each fair face as it emerged. I saw nothing then to arouse my suspicions. Yet when I went for my coat, in less than an hour, the three-cornered note was gone.

Suspicious as I was, and, for the time being, every inch of me a spy, I could fasten my suspicion upon no one person. Every girl on the ground, so far as I could hear, was talking of Deedes with the shocked fascination of inquisitive innocence: it might have been any one of them. All looked at me as though they knew me for the red-handed accomplice that I was; and those to whom I was introduced tortured me unremittingly with their questions. Never I am sure was a man more visibly embarrassed; yet who upon that ground could plumb the actual depth of my discomfort? Only one young lady refrained from adding to it, and this was Miss Enid I'Anson herself. The name of Deedes never passed between us. I fancied her relief as great as mine.

We were together some time, strolling about the ground, picking up balls, and sitting on seats we had occasionally to ourselves. Miss Enid's eyes appealed to me more than ever. They were dreadfully sad, but there was cause enough for that. I only hoped—I only hoped the three-cornered note was not in her pocket. Yet she had arrived early, and changed her shoes, and never played one sett.

My part in our conversation was chiefly wilful nonsense. I had conceived a laudable ambition to make those blue eyes smile. I am ashamed to add that I rattled on until I had them full of tears. Even then I did not adopt the usual, I believe the well-bred course of ignoring what was no business of mine.

"You are in trouble," said I bluntly. "How is it at the bank?"

"My father has been summoned to Melbourne by the directors," she answered in a low voice. "My mother——"

"Your mother?" I repeated presently.

"Is ill in bed," she sobbed. "Oh, Mr. Bower, it is a dreadful, dreadful trouble! You will wonder why I am here. I am here for the best. Think that, and nothing more."

But I was not thinking of that at all; a dumb, blind rage had risen within me against the author of all this mischief; and if beforehand I was set upon my compact with Deedes, the tears of this sweet girl were as the seal and signature of my determination. Their money for his freedom; entire restitution for my risk. On any other terms I would not only be no friend to him, but his relentless foe.

Thinking of little else meanwhile, and pleading my sleepless night as an excuse alike for continued silence and for an early retreat to my lodging, I found him, shortly after nine o'clock, crouched in the cellar of the empty house, and evidently much altered by his long day in hiding. He said it had seemed like a week; and the few minutes, during which some fellow had been poking about the place, like a day. I told him that was the sergeant. The men had not been to mend the window. Deedes wished they had. Any risk, he said, would have been better than the interminable waiting and the ceaseless listening. But for one little friend he had found he would have made a dash for it and chanced everything. And in the light of the candle I had brought with me, he showed me a brown mouse seated on the collar of his coat; but when I pushed the candle closer, the mouse fled with a scuttle and a squeak.

"Ah, you've frightened him," said Deedes; "however, he's done his part. It killed the afternoon, taming him; have you ever tamed anything, Beetle? I have, every kind of animal, including women; but, by George, I never expected to see myself as tame as I am to-night! I'm unmanned. I feel like the Prisoner of Chillon. I'm rusted with his vile repose. You could lift me out by the hair and give me to the nearest bobby!"

"Come," I said, "there's no need for that. Only show me where the money is, and do as you've resolved to do, and it won't be such a very bad business after all. I suppose you haven't weakened on what we said this morning?"

He laughed bitterly; it was his deep dejection that had turned away my wrath.

"Good heavens, no! Have you? Did you put those notes where I told you to? Did you get the whiskers?"

"I have done both," said I, seeing no point in mentioning the contretemps at the church. "Here are the whiskers; I bought them at a hairdresser's—for theatricals. And here's a clean duck suit and a helmet that I used to wear at sea. Don't look askance at them. I know they're conspicuous. For that very reason, they're going to nip suspicion in the bud."

Deedes considered a moment, and then gave the most genuine laugh I had heard from him yet.

"By George, they're the very thing!" he cried, in a soft enthusiasm. "Lend me your hand, Beetle, for I'm as stiff as the dead."

Five minutes later he rustled and gleamed from his chin to his ankles in snowy whites; blonde whiskers wept from either cheek; then with his pen-knife he hacked at his moustache until his mouth showed through and spoilt him; and with that we were ready to start. Our rendezvous was Western Beach; our only difficulty, an unseen exit from the house. We had luck, however, on our side. Not only did we break covert unobserved, but we met with no undue scrutiny in the open; not a single constable saw or was seen of us. So we gained the beach, deeply grateful to our proper stars.

"Now," said Deedes, "you follow me along this pier."

"Why?" said I, with ugly visions; and instinctively I stood in my tracks.

"Why? You see that topsail schooner away along on the left? Well, I haven't told you before, but that's where the swag is—aboard the schooner *Mollyhawk*—waiting for me!"

"I'm not coming," said I stoutly. "You're a desperate man, Deedes. I know you; none of your hanky-panky. Go you and fetch it. I stay where I am."

"My good fellow, it's far too heavy for one to carry. There's hundreds and hundreds in gold!"

"Then bring your accomplice. I'm not frightened of you!" said I fiercely. "I see a man within a hundred yards; he's coming this way; I shall have him by to see fair-play."

"Oh, call him then!" cried Deedes, with an oath. "No," he added with another, "I'll do it for you. Not to trust a fellow in a mess like this!"

It was a very low cry that he uttered, but the man came up in a moment. I was surprised that he had heard it at all, surprised also but more puzzled by a something familiar in his size and gait. And yet not until he was up with us, and shaking hands with Deedes, did I recognise my burly adversary of the church hard at hand.

"Help! help!" I cried, with sudden insight.

"My dear old chap, what nonsense!" said Deedes, throwing an arm round my neck. Something was pressed across my mouth—something moist and cool like a dog's nose—and held there, as I was held, while sense and strength ebbed out together. Then the masts and spars of ships flew to the stars in a soundless explosion; and I knew no more.

IV

I awoke between clean sheets in a narrow, natty berth. I had been stripped to the singlet, and yet handled with evident kindness. My clothes hung tidily from a peg; they were swaying very gently to and fro, like the candle-stick in its socket, and the curtains of my bunk. I was aboard the *Mollyhawk*, and the *Mollyhawk* was out at sea. I bounded to the floor, to the port; it was open, and I looked out into the alleyway. They had imprisoned me, then, in a deck-house stateroom. I made no doubt the door was locked, tried it, found it unlocked; had a vision of white napery and bright silver in the saloon; and closed the door more calmly than I had opened it. I realised that I was in the hands of a deliberate, cool, resourceful rascal; my only weapons, therefore, were coolness, deliberation, and resource.

So I dressed myself with care, and ere I was ready, could smile at the simple wiles which had ensnared me: the two farewell letters, of which one, alas! was evidently genuine; the well-acted depression and the air of resigned defeat at the close of a long day in loathly hiding. These pretences, so transparent now, struck no shame to my heart as I recalled them; for I knew that, were it all to come over again, I should be again deceived. What was must be endured; it was of no use thinking about it; one must think of what might yet be done. But where were we—through the Heads? By the gentle, joyful motion it was impossible to tell. Had we shown our heels? And for what port in all the world were we bound? As if in answer, the tramp of feet and the sound of rough voices in unison came to me at that moment through the open port:

"O where are you going to, my pretty maid?
Wa-ay, Rio!

O where are you going to, my pretty maid?
We're bound for Rio Grande!"

I had learnt and liked the chanty on my voyage out in the Glasgow clipper; and half involuntarily, half out of bravado, I was joining in the chorus when I appeared on deck. I even lent a hand at the capstan, as Deedes had done himself, and I had the satisfaction of silencing his voice with the first note of my own:

"An' it's he-ey, Rio!
Wa-ay, Rio!
Sing fare you well,
You bonny young gell,
We're bound for——"

"Belay!" cried the jolly rich voice of that great villain, my churchyard acquaintance of Western Beach. As our eyes met, he honoured me with a jovial nod; then my white duck suit came between us, a little creased, but spotless as on the night before; and Deedes was looking me up and down.

"You're a cool hand, too," said he. "Well, I'm blowed!"

"I am studying in a cool school," said I. "Deedes, I admire you; more than ever; there!"

"That's very nice of you, Beetle."

"Not a bit; it won't prevent me from getting even with you the first chance I see."

"You'll find that difficult."

"I shall stick at nothing."

His face darkened. He had shaved himself clean since the night, and as he showed me his teeth I thought I had never seen so vile a mouth. It had degenerated dreadfully since his boyhood.

"Take care," he snarled; "you're being done pretty well so far. You've the second best stateroom aboard, and the cuddy tucker's all right. Don't you forget we've got a hold and irons, and rats and rancid pork as well!"

He turned on his heel, and I walked to the binnacle. Next moment he joined me there, dropping a hand upon my shoulder.

"East-by-south-a-quarter-east," said he; "we cleared the Heads last night—bound for Rio Grande, or something like it—and that chunk on the port bow is Wilson Promontory. So now you know. And look here, Beetle, old chap, you've been good to me; I don't want to be rough on you. Did you really think I was going to do as we said? My good fellow, how could you? See here, Beetle: the yacht's a well-known yacht, Watson's a well-known yachtsman, and he was in Melbourne to divert suspicion the day I did the trick. He stands in for his share. Why not stand in yourself? You've earned your little bit, if anybody has!"

"I thought you didn't want to be rough on me," said I wearily. "Have you got it all aboard?"

"Have I not! Every penny-piece!"

"And who's Watson?"

I was at once introduced to the marine monster in blue, with the superfluous comment, "I believe you've met before. Captain Watson owns and skips this ship, and I skip and own the money; I'm purser, so to speak, but there'll be fair do's at the end of the voyage. You'd much better stand in, Beetle. The captain and I are both quite clear on the point."

"Oh, so am I," cried I ironically. "When one of you two has knifed the other for his share, I intend sticking the one who's left!"

"I consider that remark," said the captain, colouring, "in the worst of taste; and if you weren't a friend of Mr. Deedes, I should kick you off my quarter-deck."

Mr. Deedes looked thunderous, but said nothing.

"Oh, come," said I, "if we can't have our joke what can we have? I admit, if there'd been any truth in what I said—any chance or possibility of truth—I should have merited a visitation from the captain's boots; but as I was talking arrant nonsense, what did it matter?"

I expected a blow for that, and tried to look as though I did not, being extremely anxious to return it with effect. I was, in fact, the slave all this time of emotional cross-currents, which made my revulsion from these villains the stronger because it was not continuous. I had more than tolerated them at first, but all at once I found myself desiring hold and rats and irons, rather than a continuance of their society. At this moment, however, the old and evil-looking steward was to be seen carrying smoking dishes to the house; the sight appealed to me in another place; and I will own to having changed my manner with some abruptness, and to adding an apologetic word on top of that.

"All right," said Deedes savagely. "You've said about enough, and in the cuddy I'll trouble you to hold your tongue altogether. The mate's asleep in the other stateroom—take care you don't lose yours! Take jolly good care this isn't your first and last meal up here!"

After breakfast I smoked a pipe in the cross-trees, and looked in vain for a passing funnel: only a few insignificant sails were in sight, and those to leeward. The sea lay under me like a great blue plate, the schooner a white ant crawling in its centre. But for the swell, we might have been in Corio Bay. Should I ever see it again, I wondered, with the straight streets sloping to its brink? And I wondered if Deedes had the same thought, as he leant over the taffrail studying the wake; or had he more pangs and fears than he pretended, and were we less safe?

The captain joined him, whereupon Deedes retreated to the house, with black looks that were blacker still a few minutes later when he returned. Instead of rejoining the captain, he now came aloft to my cross-trees, and I made up my mind that we were to have it out in mid-air. Deedes passed me, however, without a word, and I saw a telescope sticking out of his pocket as he climbed higher. I thought it as well to let him have the mast to himself, and left him sweeping the horizon from near the truck.

Yet my own eyes were pretty good, and they had descried no sign of sail or smoke to windward. Why then this change in Deedes? Thoroughly puzzled, I reached the deck and strolled idly to the house; and the puzzle solved itself even as I entered and saw who was seated at the table.

"Miss I'Anson!" I fairly shouted.

"Yes—it is I. He said I should not see you. Do go—do go before he comes!"

"Go!" I cried. "Not see you! I shall see you and stay with you until I'm dragged out by force. That is"—I added suddenly—"unless you are here of your own free will. In that case——"

"No, no!" cried the girl. "By trickery! By wicked, heartless, abominable lies! Nothing else—oh, nothing else would have brought me to this!"

"Then we're in the same boat with a vengeance," said I, seating myself on the opposite side of the table. "Tell me how it happened—and quickly. He has talked already of putting me in irons; he'll do it after this."

"Oh, where am I to begin? There is so much to tell—but he shall not do it!" vowed Miss I'Anson. "He shall not separate the only two honest people in the ship! Oh, yes, it was lies, but lies so clever and so fiendish! Let me tell you everything. I'll try to be quick. He has been in the bank about a year. You know him perhaps better than I do. They say you were at school

- 80 -

together. You must know his good points, Mr. Bower. I mean the points that would attract a girl. They attracted me. I made a fool of myself. You must have heard about it in Geelong. Well, it's quite true; but it wasn't yesterday, or the day before, or last week. It was in the very beginning. I got over it long ago. But he has always fascinated me. You know him—you can understand? Well, when the bank was robbed I knew he had done it; I can't tell you how I knew, but know I did. His voice was not real. I have been made love to in that voice—there! Well, I went to his rooms. He lunched there every day. I saw his landlady. He had come in to lunch as usual, and said he would ring when he wanted his pudding. He did ring, but was longer than usual in ringing; that was all. His room was the back-room of the house on the ground-floor; the landlady lives in front. Quite a short time ago it was the other way about, and he suggested the alteration. He also made her promise to keep the blinds down in the kitchen, and the windows shut, to keep out the flies and the sun in the heat of the day; he could make her do what he liked. Now listen. The bank garden adjoins his landlady's garden. I found soil on his window-sill, soil on the woodwork. This was in the afternoon when the excitement was at its height; he was in the bank. I came away, making the woman promise not to say a word; but she broke her promise that night, and that was what started the hue and cry. Meanwhile I wrote him a note telling him I knew all, refusing to see him, but solemnly undertaking that if he would put a note where he had once put other notes (because my mother couldn't endure him), and say in it where the money was, nobody should ever know from me that he had touched it. Remember, Mr. Bower, I was once fond of him; nay, you did much as I did yourself; you will understand. He has told me all that has passed between you; how he gave you the note to put in the tennis pavilion. And what do you think he said in it? That if I would come to the beach at ten last night he would tell me where the money was. He did tell me. He told me it was sunk among the rocks at Queenscliff. He told me he was escaping in the *Mollyhawk*—this vessel—but he would land me at Queenscliff, and show me where the place was; because he meant to take the gold, but the notes he dare not. It was the notes that mattered to my father and the bank. They were nine-tenths of the stolen sum. Oh, I know I was a fool to believe or listen to a word he said! I should have had him put in prison at the first. But I am punished as I deserve; they will never forgive me at home; it will break their hearts; they will never get over it. And here I am—and here I am!"

She broke down, breathless, and I glanced towards the door. Deedes stood there in my ducks, his face the blacker by contrast; he glared at me, and his evil mouth worked spasmodically; but now more than ever I seemed to discern some foreign trouble in his blazing eyes; and instead of ordering me out of the deck-house, he slammed the door upon us both. Enid I'Anson whipped her face from her hands.

"That's all right," said I. "He's seen us, and he doesn't care. There's something else upon his nerves; when thieves fall out, you know—perhaps they've done so already. I feel hopeful; it's bound to come. There's just one thing I don't size down. I know why I am here: he wouldn't kill me, and alive on land I'd never have let him clear the Heads. That's why I'm here; but why are you? You didn't know about the schooner?"

"No, but—how can I tell you!"

"Don't," said I, for she was clearly in a new distress.

"I must! He wants to marry me—so he says. He never wanted before. But I did not betray him. I have saved him—he will have it so—so I am to be his wife! Oh, Mr. Bower, it is the worst insult of all! I told him so, just before you came in."

"Then that was the trouble," said I. "It rather disappoints me; I am counting on a row between those two. But it will come. Cheer up, Miss I'Anson; let him leave me out of irons twenty-four hours longer, and I'll play a hand myself—for you and the bank!"

And so I talked, trying with all my might to comfort the poor child in her extremity. She was little more; nineteen, she told me. There were elder sisters married, and a brother gone home to Cambridge. He would have to leave there now; and who would pay his passage back to Melbourne? The robbery seemed to spell certain ruin to the I'Ansons, at all events in their own belief; but now at least we knew who had drawn the cartridges from the bank revolver; and I fancy they all exaggerated the element of personal responsibility.

I did my best to reassure Miss Enid on the point; nor did I leave a comfortable word unsaid that I could hit upon. So noon, and afternoon, found us talking still across the cuddy table. Luncheon in this pirate's craft was evidently a movable feast, to-day indefinitely postponed. Enid looked at her watch and found it after three o'clock; we had thought it one; but about half-past three the house door was flung open and in strode Deedes. He did not look at us, but snatched a repeating-rifle out of a locker, and would have gone without a word but for Enid I'Anson.

The girl was terrified. "What are you going to do with it?" she cried; and he paused in the doorway, filling it with his broad shoulders, so that I could see nothing but blue sky without.

"There's a big bird in our wake—another mollyhawk!" said Deedes, as I thought with a lighter look. "I'm going to have pots at it. That's all."

"Cruel always," said the girl, as we heard shot after shot in quick succession. But I went to the door, and then turned back as if with an altered mind. I had found it locked.

Ere I could regain my seat, a new thing happened. A bullet came clean through the deck-house, passed over Enid's head, and must have abode in my brain had I sat a minute longer where I had been sitting for hours.

"Coward!" gasped the girl; but only with her word came the report.

"A chase!" I shouted. "Down on the floor with you—flat down—that was a Government bullet!" And on the cabin floor we crouched.

Voices hailing us were now plainly audible. But Deedes vouchsafed no answer, save with his Winchester, and from the spitting of a revolver (doubtless handled by the captain) I gathered we were at pretty close quarters. So the chase had been going on for hours; that was why we two in the house had been left undisturbed and dinnerless; but what amazed me most was the evident good discipline on deck. We must stand some chance; my soul sickened at the thought. It must be canvas that was after us, not steam; but I could not look out to see; my brave comrade would only remain where she was on condition I did the same. Lastly, every man aboard the schooner, myself excepted, must centre his hopes, perhaps his designs, upon the nineteen thousand and odd pounds that lay snug somewhere between her keelson and her trucks.

I have done livelier things than lie there listening to the shots; many more had struck the house, and even where we lay there was no superfluous safety; but my comrade bore herself throughout with incredible spirit, and made besides a sweet, strange picture, there on that matted floor. The sun streamed in through the skylight, and the schooner's motion was such that the girl's face was now bathed in the rays and anon lighted only by its own radiance. I did not know how I liked it best; nor do I to this day, though I see her always as I saw her then. Her blue eyes bent on mine the kind of look which would give one courage in one's last hour. Her very hand was cool.

The firing on both sides continued intermittently; but once we heard a heavy thud upon our own deck, and the revolver spat no more.

"That's not Deedes," said I, shaking my head; "I only wish it was!"

"Don't say that," my comrade answered; "it would be too dreadful! He is not fit to die; he has fine qualities—you know it yourself—he could play a man's part yet in the world."

Even as she spoke the door was unlocked, flung open, and Deedes himself stood looking down upon us across his folded arms. I daresay we cut an ignominious figure enough, crouching there upon the cabin floor. Deedes looked very sick and pale, but the sight of us elicited a sardonic smile.

"Get up," said he. "There will be no more fighting. Watson's knocked out. I've struck my flag. Your father will be aboard in a minute, Enid."

"My father!"

"Yes," said Deedes, leaning back against a bulkhead, with his arms still folded. "It's a pilot's cutter—the first thing handy, I suppose—with the police and your father aboard her. One word before he comes. Once you'd have come fast enough to my arms. Enid—I'm done for—come to them now!"

He unfolded and flung them wide as he spoke; a great look lit his face, half mocking, half sublime, and down my duck jacket, where his arms had been, a dark stream trickled to the deck. Before I could get to him he fell in a white heap under our eyes.

*   *   *   *   *   *   *   *

Deedes was dead. Watson was dying. Two constables in the cutter were badly hit; and with their ghastly burden the little ships tacked home in consort to Port Philip Heads.

It was midnight when we saw the lights. The bank-manager and I stood together on the cutter's deck, he with a brace of heavy bags between his heels. His daughter was down below, but the thought of her troubled him still. As he said, the money was the bank's, and it was safe; but his daughter was his own, and this scandal would attach forever to her name. I denied it hotly, but the old man would have it so.

"Don't tell me," he grumbled. "I know the world, and Enid will go ashore with something unpleasantly like a slur upon her name."

"Then it won't be for long," I at last retorted. "We meant it to keep until we got there; but with your permission, sir, your daughter and I shall go ashore engaged."

THE VOICE OF GUNBAR

"H'sh! Did you hear a coo-ee?"

I shook my head in some surprise. My host seemed a good fellow; but hitherto he had proved an extremely poor companion, and for five minutes, I suppose, neither of us had said a word. My eyes had fallen from the new well, with its pump and white palings shining like ivory under the full moon, to our two shadows skewered through and through by those of the iron hurdles against which we were leaning. These hurdles enclosed and protected a Moreton Bay fig, which had been planted where the lid of the old well used to lie, so I had just been told; and I had said I wondered why one well should have been filled in and another sunk so very near the same place, and getting no answer I had gone on wondering for those five minutes. So if there had been any sound beyond the croaking of the crickets (which you get to notice about as much as the tick of a clock), I felt certain that I must have heard it too. I, however, was a very new chum, whereas Warburton of Gunbar was a ten-year bushman, whose ear might well be quicker than mine to catch the noises of the wilderness; and when I raised my eyes inquisitively there was a light in his that made me uneasy.

"Hear it now?" he said quietly, and with a smile, as a seaman points out sails invisible to the land-lubber. "I do—plainly."

"I don't," I candidly replied. "But if it's some poor devil lost in the mallee, you'll be turning out to look for him, and I'll lend you a hand."

His homestead, you see, was in the heart of the mallee, and on the edge of a ten-mile block which was one tangle of mallee and porcupine scrub from fence to fence. I shuddered to think of anyone being bushed in that stuff, for away down in Warburton's eyes there was a horror that had gone like a bullet to my nerves. I was therefore the more surprised at the dry laugh with which he answered:

"You'd better stop where you are."

I could not understand the man. He was not only the manager of Gunbar, but overseer and store-keeper as well, an unmarried man and a solitary. One's first impression of him was that his lonely life and depressing surroundings had sadly affected his whole nature. He had looked askance at me when I rode up to the place, making me fancy I had at last found the station where an uninvited guest was also unwelcome. After that preliminary scrutiny, however, his manner had warmed somewhat. He asked me several questions concerning the old country from which we both came; and I remember liking him for putting on a black coat for supper, which struck me as a charming conceit in that benighted spot, and not a woman within twenty-five miles of us. His latest eccentricity pleased me less. Either he was chaffing me, and he had heard nothing (but his sombre manner made that incredible), or he was prepared to let a fellow-creature perish fearfully without an attempt at rescue. I was thankful when he explained himself.

"I know who it is, you see," he said presently, striking a match on the hurdle and re-lighting his pipe. "It's all right."

"But who is it?" said I; for that would not do for me.

"It's Mad Trevor," he returned gravely. "Come now!" he added, looking me in the face much as he had done before inviting me to dismount; "do you mean to say you have got as far as this and never heard the yarn of Mad Trevor of Gunbar?"

I made it clear that I knew nothing at all about it; and in the end he told me the story as we stood in the station yard, and lounged against those iron hurdles right under the great round moon.

"My lad, I was as young as you are when I came to this place; but that's very near ten years ago, and ten years take some time in the mallee scrub. Yes, I know I look older than that; but this country would age anybody, even if nothing happened to start your white hairs before their time. I'm going to tell you what did happen within my first two months on this station. Mad Trevor was manager then, and he and I were to run the show between us as soon as I knew my business. To learn it, I used to run up the horses at five o'clock in the morning, and run 'em out again last thing at night, for the drought had jolly nearly dried us up, and in the yard yonder we had to give every horse his nose-bag of chaff before turning him out. Well, between sparrow-chirp and bedtime I was either mustering or boundary-riding, or weighing out rations in the store, or taking them to the huts in the spring-cart, or making up the books, or sweeping out my store, or cleaning up the harness; but I never had ten minutes to myself, for old Trevor believed in making me work all the harder because I was only to get my tucker for it till I knew the ropes. And for my part I'm bound to say I thoroughly enjoyed the life in those days, as I daresay you do now. The rougher the job, the readier was I to tackle it. So I think the boss was getting to like me, and I know I liked him; but for all that, he was mad, as I soon found out from the men, who had christened him Mad Trevor.

"It appeared that he had come to Gunbar some three or four years before me, with his young wife and their baby girl, Mona, who was five years old when first I saw her—riding across this very yard on her father's shoulders. Ay, and I can see her now, with her yellow head of hair and her splendid little legs and arms! She was forever on Mad Trevor's back, or in his arms, or on his knee, or at his side in the buggy, or even astride in front of him on the saddle-bow; and her father's face beaming over her shoulder, and his great beard tickling her cheeks, and he watching her all the time with the tenderest love that ever I saw in human eyes. For, you see, the wife had died here on Gunbar, and lay buried in the little cemetery we have behind the stock-yards; but she was going to live again in little Mona; and Trevor knew that, and was just waiting.

"But his trouble had driven him quite mad; for often I have been wakened when I'd just dropped off, by hearing him come down the verandah trailing his blanket after him; and away he was gone to camp all night on his wife's grave. The men used to hear him talking to her up there; it would have made your heart bleed for him, he was such a rough-and-ready customer with all of us but the child.

"Well, one day we were out on the run together, he and I in the buggy. It was to fix a new rope round the drum of the twelve-mile whim—at the far side of the mallee, that is—and I recollect he showed me how it was done that day so that I never needed showing again, and it was because I was quickish at picking up such things that he liked me. But a brute of a dust-storm came on just as we finished, and we had to wait at the whim-driver's hut till it was over; and that was the first time I ever heard him mention little Mona's name behind her back. For the whim-driver had a fine coloured print, from some Christmas number, stuck up over his bunk, and it was a treat to hear the poor boss beg it from him to bring home to the little one. It was as though the bare thought of the kid made a difference in the look of his eye and the tone of his voice; for he had been swearing at the rope and us in his best style; but he never swore once on the drive back, he only made me hold the rolled print in my hand the whole time; and I had to take tremendous care of it, and hand it over to him the moment we pulled up in the yard here, so that he might give it to little Mona first thing. But that was not to be: the child was lost. She had been missing since the time of the dust-storm, which was mid-day, and all hands but the cook who told us, and the nurse who was responsible and beside herself, were out searching for her already.

"The boss took the news without immediately getting down from the buggy, and with none of the bluster which he usually had ready for the least thing. But his face was all hair and freckles, and I recollect how the freckles stood out when he turned to speak to me; and to this day I can feel the pinch of his fingers on the fleshy part of my arm.

"'Harry,' he says, in a kind of whisper, 'you must turn these two out, and then run up Blücher and Wellington; and you must drive that nurse girl away from this, Harry—you must take her away this very night. For if my child is dead, I'll kill her too—by God, but I will!'

"But the nurse had seen us drive up, and as Mad Trevor crossed the yard heavily, like a dazed man, she ran out from the verandah and threw herself at his knees, sobbing her heart out. What he said to her first I couldn't catch: I only know that in another moment he was crying like a child himself. No wonder either, when the mallee is the worst kind of scrub to get lost in, and there had been enough dust to clean out deeper tracks than a child's, and when it was growing late in the afternoon, and the poor little thing out for hours already. But it was the most pitiful sight you ever saw— the servant girl in hysterics and the poor old boss steadying his voice to take the blame off her he'd said he'd kill. Ay, he was standing just in front of the verandah, within three yards of where we are now, and that rolled-up print was still in his hand.

"So no more was said about my carting the poor girl off that night; but Wellington and Blücher were run up all the same, and at sundown they were bowling the buggy away back to the twelve-mile with me in her. You see, the twelve-mile whim-driver was Gunbar George, our oldest hand, who knew every inch of the run, so the boss thought that George would lay hold of little Mona sooner than he could, if she was in the mallee. And that's where she was, we were all quite certain; and George was certain too, when I told him; and he told of a man he himself had once found in our mallee, stone-dead, with 'died from thirst' scratched in the grime on the bottom of his quart pot, and all within a mile of this very homestead.

"That wasn't a pretty story to leave behind with a new chum who was going to camp alone in a lonely hut for the first time of asking, and nothing to think about but the poor little bairn that was lost. I tell you, I shall remember that night as long as I live, and how I felt when I had seen the last of George and the buggy in the moonlight; for by that time it was night, and just such another as this, with the moon right overhead, as round as an orange, and not a cloud in the sky. Ah! we have plenty of nights like that in the back-blocks, and one full moon is as like the last as two peas, for want of clouds; and somehow they always seem to come before they're due; yet it's a weary while to look back upon, with that night at the end of all, like a gate after five miles of posts and wire. Say now—have you never heard him all this time?" He had paused, with his head bent and on one side.

I replied that I had heard nothing but his story; that what I wanted to hear was the end of it, and that Mad Trevor would keep. He smiled when I said that, and stood listening for another minute or more, with his eyes drawn back into his head.

"Ah, well!" he tossed up his head and went on, "it came to an end in time, like most nights; but the worst was before it began, when I could hear George cracking his whip whenever I stood still. So I stood still until I knew I should hear him no more, and then I blew up the fire for my tea, for I had a fair twist after all that driving. But Lord, you'll hear how your boots creak the first time you camp alone in a hut—especially if it's a good one with a floor to it like our twelve-mile! I tell you I took mine off, and then I put 'em on again, because my stocking-soles made just as much noise in their own way, and it was a creepier way. Then there are two or three rooms to the hut out there—it's a fine hut, our twelve-mile—and I had to poke my nose into them all before I could tackle my tea. And then I had to walk right round the hut in the moonlight, as if it had been a desert island. But it was lighter outside than in, for I had nothing but a slush-lamp—you know, a strip of moleskin in a tin of mutton fat—and I didn't understand the working of one in those days any better than I suppose you would now. Well, then, the whim-water at the twelve-mile is brackish, so I had to fill the billy at an open tank that was getting low; but there'd been a tantalising little shower of sixty points a day or two before that had made the water muddy; and I very well remember that the billy looked full of tea before I opened my hand to slip the tea in. Then the hut was swarming with bull-ants, and they came crawling up the sides of the billy and into the tea where I had set it to cool on the floor; and the light was so bad that I had to chance those ants, because you couldn't tell them from tea-leaves. Well, I could have enjoyed the experience, and thought of the fine letter home it would have made, if I hadn't been thinking all the time of that poor little thing in the mallee. I was just about as new a chum as you are now, and there was a kind of interest in turning my pouch inside out for the last pipeful of the cut-up tobacco I had brought up with me from Melbourne. It was one of the last fills of cut-up that ever I had until you handed me your pouch to-night, because when you once get used to the black cakes you'll find you'll stick to them. So there I sat and smoked my pipe on the doorstep, and kept looking at the moon, and thinking of the old people in the old country, and wishing they could see me just then. I daresay you think like that sometimes, but you'll find you get over that too. It was worse to think of that little mite in the mallee scrub, and how she had sat on my knee the night before; and how she would come into my store when I was doing the books, spill the flour about, and keep on asking questions. That's the store over there, at the other side of the new well, with the bell on top and the narrow verandah in front. I must show you little Mona's height on the centre post: I had to measure her every morning after once getting her to bed by telling her she only grew in her sleep.

"Well, thinking wouldn't do any good, and my last pipe of cut-up was soon done, for it was nothing but powder. I had brought a cake of the black stuff with me, but it was too strong for me in those days. So then I thought I had better turn in, though it was only ten o'clock; so I took my blanket and the slush-lamp to the little dark room at the back, and pulled off my coat and boots, and spread my blanket on George's bunk. And before I lay down— well, I thought I should like to put in a prayer for the poor little thing that was lost; and I reckon it was about the last time I was ever on my knees at that business, for you'll find these back-blocks don't make a man more religious than he need be. But it was a comfort to me that night; and, while I was kneeling, a little kitten of George's, that I'd never noticed when I first looked into the room, came out and went for my stocking-soles; and that was another comfort, I tell you! Mind you, I was twelve miles from a house, and five from the nearest fellow-creature, a boundary-rider on the next run. I had never been able to get that out of my head, so the kitten was a godsend, and though he would come on to the bed to tickle my toes, I wouldn't have been without him for all I was worth. I had a paper too— one of my home papers that I hadn't had time to read; and I stuck up the slush-lamp, and strained my eyes at the print until I couldn't keep them open any longer; and what with the kitten, that was purring very loud at my feet (but the louder he made it the homelier it sounded), I found myself tumbling off to sleep long before I had expected to, and in better heart too.

"I suppose I must have slept for some hours, for when I woke the moon was low and swollen, and hanging like a Chinese lantern in the very middle of my open doorway. But I never looked at my watch; I lay there staring at the setting moon, and listening for a repetition of the sound that had roused me. I had not long to wait, but yet long enough to make me wonder at the time whether I mightn't have heard it in my dreams only. And then it came again—the long-drawn wail, the piercing final cry of a coo-ee from one that had learnt to coo-ee before he could speak. As my feet touched the floor I heard another coo-ee; as I ran out into the moonshine there came a fourth; but the fifth was in my ear before I knew that they all came from the mallee scrub that spreads westward from here to within half a mile of the twelve-mile whim. Then I answered as well as I knew how; but the acquirement was a very recent one in my case; and besides, my wits were still in a tangle. For first I thought it was the child herself, until I realised, with a laugh at the absurdity of the idea, that she could neither walk so far nor coo-ee like that; and then I supposed it must be some chance traveller that had got bushed, like others before him, in that deadly mallee. But all the while I was answering his coo-ees as best I could, and running in my socks in the direction from which they seemed to come. And long before I spied my man I made sure that it was Mad Trevor himself, for I knew no other with such lungs, and who else would have searched for a bairn of five so many weary miles from the spot where it had last been seen?

"But, as a matter of fact, he himself had no notion where he was, until he saw me standing in front of him in the low moonlight. Then he wanted to know what I meant by coming back from the twelve-mile; for, don't you see, he thought he had been coasting around the home-station all night— and that'll tell you about our mallee! When I set him right he just stood there, wringing his big hands like a woman; and it was worse to see than when he cried like a child before the little one's nurse.

"Of course I got him to come back with me to the hut; and he leant on my shoulder with his sixteen stone, and he just said, 'Well, Harry, I don't believe she's in the mallee at all. I've been coo-eeing for her the whole night, ever since you went; and George has been coo-eeing for her ever since he came; and all hands have been coo-eeing for her in the mallee all night long. And I don't believe she's there at all. I believe she's somewhere about the homestead all the time. We never looked there. What fools we all are. You shall make me a pannikin of tea, and I'll turn in and have a sleep, Harry; and we'll go back together when it's light; and we'll find her asleep in the chaff-house, I shouldn't wonder, if they haven't found her already; you bet we'll find her safe and sound in some hole or corner, the rogue! frightening her old dad out of all his wits.'

"And indeed, as he spoke, he gave a mad laugh even for him; and I shrank away from under his great hand, that would keep tightening on my shoulder; and left him to sit down in the hut while I went to the wood-heap, and then to the tank to rinse and refill the billy.

"But that notion of his about the homestead had been my notion too, in a kind of way; only I had kept it to myself because they were all so cock-sure it was the mallee, and they would know best. I was thinking it out, though, as I chopped the wood, and thinking it out as I rinsed the billy. Now, to do this where the water was clearest, I had to lean over from a bit of a staging, the tank being low, as I told you. But this time, through thinking so much more of Mona than of what I was doing, I lost my balance, and very nearly toppled in. And then I had to think no more, for in a flash I knew where little Mona was."

The instant he paused I saw him listening. He was standing in front of me now, but my back was still to the little fig-tree, and my hands had the hurdle tight. I neither spoke nor took my eyes off him till he went on.

"Yes, she was under the ground you're standing on," said Warburton, nodding his head as I started from the place; "she had fallen into the old well, and pulled down the lid in trying to save herself. I knew it at the moment I was near toppling into the twelve-mile tank that wasn't one foot deep. It turned out to be so. But I was never surer of it than when I went back to the hut, spilling the water the whole way, I was in such a tremble. And the difficulty was to keep the knowledge—for knowledge it was— from the poor boss; it had cheered him so to think the child had never been near the mallee! Why, before daylight he dozed off quite comfortably on George's bunk in my blanket; and I sat and watched him, and listened to him snoring; and could have fetched the axe from the wood-heap and brained him where he lay, so that he might never know.

"And he took it so calmly after all! I do assure you, when we had buried her alongside her mother, he stood where we are now, and set all hands digging the new well and filling in the old, and swore at us like a healthy man when we didn't do this or that his way. It was he who designed those palings, and would have no more lids, but a pump; though there was neither woman nor child on the station to meet with accidents now, but only us men. And he was smoking his pipe when he planted this fig, for I was by at the time, and remember him telling me his wife had brought it from Moreton Bay in Queensland. I had seen it often in a pot, and now I had to say whether it was plumb; and with his pipe in his mouth and his head on one side he seemed as callous as you please. And for three weeks, to my certain knowledge, he slept every night in his room, and I would have thought nothing of sleeping there with him, he was bearing it so grandly. Then came the full moon and the bright nights again; and we heard him in the mallee, coo-eeing for the child that lay beside her mother—him that had buried them both!

"Well, he didn't come back next morning, so now all hands turned out to search for *him*. But we never found him all day, for he had crossed his tracks again and again; and all next night we heard him coo-eeing away for his dead child, but now his coo-ee was getting hoarse; and God knows why, but none of us could manage to set eyes on him. It was I who found him the day after. He was lying under a hop-bush, but the sun had shifted and was all over him. His lips were black, and I felt certain he was dead. But when I sung out he jumped clean to his feet, with his fists clenched and his red beard blowing in the hot wind, and his face and his eyes on fire. And if he had never been mad before, he was then.

"He opened his mouth, and I expected a roar, but I couldn't understand a word he said until he had half emptied my water-bag.

"'What do you want with me?' he says at last; and of course I said I wanted him to come back to the station with me. So he says, 'You leave me alone—don't you meddle with me. I'm not coming back till I find my little 'un that's bushed in this mallee.' So then I saw there was nothing for it but firmness, and I said he must come with me—as if it had been poor wee

Mona herself. But he only laughed and swore, and went on warning me not to meddle with him. Well, I was just forced to. But sixteen stone takes a lot of weakening, and the last I saw of him alive was his great freckled fist coming at my head. I went down like a pithed bullock. And it was I who found him again the week after, when he must have been all but a week dead—but I had heard him coo-eeing every blessed night!"

He was listening again: whenever he paused, I caught him listening. I was still to understand it, and the deep-down scare in his eyes.

"Stop a bit!" said I. "Don't tell me he's dead if he's only mad, and you've got him in some hut somewhere. You say you can hear him coo-eeing—I see you can."

Warburton of Gunbar heaved the saddest sigh I have ever heard.

"I hear him always," he said quietly, "when the moon is at the full. I have done, all along, and it's close on ten years ago now. It's in the mallee I hear him, just as he heard little Mona; yet they all three lie together over yonder behind the stock-yards. H'sh, man, h'sh!" He was gripping at my arm, but I twisted away from him even as himself from Mad Trevor, because his listening eyes were more than enough for me. "There's his coo-ee again!" he cried, raising a hand that never quivered. "Mean to tell me you can't hear it now?"

THE MAGIC CIGAR

It was one of such a hundred as seldom find their way to the back-blocks of New South Wales. And the box was heralded by the following letter, written at a London club in the depth of winter, and read by me in my shirt-sleeves some few weeks later, as I rode home to the station with our weekly mail:—

"DEAR OLD BOY,—A Merry Christmas to you, and may the Lord give you wisdom with the New Year, that you don't spend much of it in such an infernal hole as your station seems to be. I'm particularly exercised about the baccy like shoe-leather, which you cut up for yourself before every pipe. I fear it may have a demoralising effect, so am sending you a Christmas box of decent cigars. Don't treasure them, old chap, but smoke the whole lot between Christmas and New Year, and if you like 'em send for more from your affectionate brother

"CHARLES."

Charles was a trump; but he had reckoned without the colonial tariff. I had to get a friend in Sydney to go to the custom-house for me, and I paid pretty heavily for my cigars before they ultimately reached me about the middle of January. However, they were well worth the money and the delay; for the dear good fellow had sent me a box of Villar-y-Villar (Excepcionales Rothschild) to waste their costly fragrance upon the drought-stricken wilds of Riverina.

You should have seen us when we opened the box, the manager and I. It was the cool of the evening in the homestead verandah, yet there was not wind enough to shake the flame of a vesta. We brought out the kerosine lamp, set it down on the edge of the verandah, and seated ourselves one on each side, with our feet in the sand of the station yard, and the cigar-box also between us. Reverently we raised the lid with a paper-knife, and were impressed, you may be sure, to find the cigars wrapped up in silver paper, every one, and looking like so many little silver torpedoes under the lamp. Then we lit up, and leaned against the verandah posts, and blew beautiful clouds into the cloudless purple sky, and listened to the locusts, and made a bet as to whose ash would fall first, which the manager won. Altogether it was a luxurious hour, and I for one had never tasted such a cigar before. The manager, however, a native of the colony, asserted that he had often bought as good, or better, of a bush hawker, at twenty-five shillings the hundred. But I had noticed how very gingerly he removed the silver paper from what was now a few heaps of very white ash and a stump, which he was smoking, with the aid of his pen-knife, down to the last quarter-inch.

Though the gift came so late, the donor's sporting injunctions I considered as sacred, and we gave ourselves a week to finish the box in. It was heavy smoking for hard-working young men accustomed only to the pipe. I afterwards found that the manager had banked some of his share in his desk, and I did not smoke all mine myself. I kept a case in my pocket, however, and so it happened that I had cigars about me on the broiling day when I camped in the shade with the man who had the reputation of being the champion swearer of the back-blocks. He was also a capital hand with sheep, but it was his notoriously foul mouth that had made him a public character, and throughout the district he was known as Hell-fire Jim.

We had met neither by accident nor design, but all by reason of the incredibly long range of Jim's language at its worst: on this occasion he must have brought me down at several hundred yards. Not that it was more than a voice that reached me first, for I was cantering to his assistance when the words caused me to draw rein and to marvel. It is one thing to use strong language in wild places where it is impossible to enforce your meaning without recourse to the local convention; to curse dumb animals in the silent bush, as Jim was doing when I came up with him, is surely different and peculiar. Yet I found him in provoking plight: wrestling in the thick of the scrub with some twenty weak sheep. The sheep were camping under the trees in twos and threes. Jim was galloping from one group to another with the perspiration dripping from his nose and beard and imprecations hurtling from his mouth; but it was impossible for a mere man on horseback to round up that mob among those trees, or to manage them at all; and Jim's dog was skulking and lolling its tongue, good for nothing for want of water.

That was where I had come in. My water-bag was nearly full; his had sprung a leak and was empty. To give the dog a drink out of his wide-awake was the boundary-rider's first act when I handed him my bag; then he took a pull himself. The suggestion that we should off-saddle and do a spell together came from me. The dog had found its voice and rounded up the mob before Jim finished drinking; we set him to watch the sheep in the shade, tethered our horses, and carried our saddles to a tree apart, leaving marks like inkstains on the animals' backs. The place was a sandy gully thickly timbered with pines. We chose the tree with the closest warp and woof of shadow underneath, and there made short work of such provisions as we carried, with further reductions in the bulk of my water-bag.

It was the very hottest day I can remember in the bush; in the shade of the homestead verandah the thermometer touched 116°; and I recollect my companion showing me a tear in his moleskins, done that morning by a pine-branch, and the little triangle of exposed skin on which an hour's sun had left the mark of a mustard leaf. The fellow was near to physical perfection, a sterling specimen of the Saxon type, with the fair skin which naturally burns red; but his blue eyes were sunken, and had the strange rickety look of one who has drunk both deep and long at some period of his life. Jim still knocked down his cheque, but not oftener or with worse effects than another. We regarded him, however, as our biggest blackguard, and as such he interested me, so that my eye was on him as we ate: I afterwards remembered his way of eating.

Our snack over, Jim had his cutty in his mouth and was paring a plug of black tobacco before I thought of my cigars. He laughed and swore as I produced the case, but when I opened it, and the silver cones stuck out under his nose, he helped himself without a word. His easy method of slipping off the silver paper (which had visibly embarrassed the manager of our station), and the way the boundary-rider held out his hand for my knife, are two more things which struck one later. The shape of that sun-chapped hand is a third. Heaven knows I was not consciously observant at the time. I rolled over on my back, my saddle for a pillow, and took to sending up soft, chastening clouds into the garish blue overhead. The subtle fragrance of the smoke mingled with the pungent smell of the pines, the hot still air grew rich with both; a vertical sun stabbed the fronds above us with pins and needles of dazzling light that struck to the ground like golden rain; and, but for my cigar, I had yielded to these sensuous influences and thrown it aside to close my eyes. Thus was I the slave of my luxury, but consoled myself with the thought that Jim's enjoyment would at least be heart-whole. Yet he never said so, and as we lay I could see no more of him than a single sidespring boot, a long spur, and three inches of shiny brown legging.

"You don't say how it strikes you, Jim."

"The cigar?"

"To be sure."

"Oh, it's not a bad smoke."

"No?" I raised myself on one elbow to look at the fellow. He had the cigar between his forefinger and thumb, and was blowing the most perfect rings of tobacco-smoke I ever saw.

"Yes, it's a good cigar," our boundary-rider went so far as to concede; then he replaced it between his teeth, after a moment's scrutiny with his unkempt head on one side.

"Quite sure?" I smiled.

"Quite. For my part, mind you, I prefer a good Muria—they're not so rich. It's purely a matter of taste, however, and certainly these are much more expensive."

"Indeed! Perhaps you can price them, Jim?"

"The cigar that I am smoking," said Hell-fire Jim, "would cost you a shilling at the club. If a shilling or two were an object, I suppose you could get them by the box at about ninety-two the hundred."

It was no longer what he said that astonished me, but the soft tone of his voice and the sudden absence from his conversation of the ingenious oath-combinations for which it was notorious. I sat bolt upright now, and must have shown my feelings pretty plainly, for he hastened to explain.

"I was once a waiter in a London club," he said. "That's how I know."

"Not a waiter, Jim," said I, looking him steadily in his sunken eyes. Then I begged his pardon. But Jim seemed pleased.

"Mean to say you think I was a member?"

"If you ask me, that was my idea."

"Then you were right. I was a member of several. Does it surprise you?" he added, with, I think, a rather wistful smile. I cannot be sure of that smile. His whole manner was agreeably free from sentiment.

"It doesn't surprise me a bit," I said.

"Not to find me the stump-end of a gentleman, eh?"

"No; I see that you are one."

"Was, my boy—was," corrected Jim. "I say," he went on, "this is a great cigar! You have to puff a bit to appreciate it properly."

He threw back his head and left a number of his little grey rings curling into thin air against the blue. I was not going to ask him any questions. We smoked for some time in silence. Then he exclaimed, with his eyebrows right up on his forehead, as though he himself could hardly credit it:

"Yes, by Jove! I was at Eton and the House."

"Nothing surprises me in this country," I remarked.

"Yet you're about the first that ever spotted *me*. By the way, I'm not the wicked baronet or the disguised duke, don't you know? My father's only a country squire of sorts—if he's alive. But he sent me to Eton and from there to Oxford; and from Oxford I went to the Temple, and from the Temple to the devil and all his angels. There I've stuck. And that's the genesis of Hell-fire Jimmie, if you care to know it."

I cared to know infinitely more. These crude headings were small satisfaction to me looking at the handsome sunburnt stockman and realising that I was alone in the wilderness with the romantic ruin of a noble manhood. I turned away from the quiet devil-may-care smile in the sunken blue eyes, in order to conceal the curiosity which was consuming me. I dropped back on my elbow to the ground, and stared into the unbroken unsuggestive blue of the southern summer sky. When I sucked at my cigar I discovered that I had let it out. Turning once more to my companion, I found him puffing his with the loving deliberation of a connoisseur.

"Like velvet, isn't it?" he murmured, stroking the brown leaf gently with his finger. "That's one of the points of a good cigar, and another's the ash. You never saw a firmer nor a whiter ash than this. My good fellow, it's a cigar for the gods!"

He held it admiringly at arm's length, as I relit mine. Then he smoked on in silence, but very slowly and caressingly, for some minutes longer. At length he said musingly:

"I wonder how long it is since I smoked my last cigar? How long is it since I came out here? I'm losing count of the years, and I've just about forgotten Oxford and London, and the wine and the women, and the old country altogether. All but one woman and one village.... I suppose you couldn't put a fellow in the way of forgetting *them?*"

I was still wondering what on earth to say to him—for once more I seemed to detect a wistful ring in his voice—when he settled the question himself by laughing in my face.

"How could you help me when you don't know the yarn?" he asked, with his blue eyes full of amusement. "Look here, I've a good mind to inflict it on you!"

"Wouldn't that hurt?" I could not help asking him.

"Nothing hurts now," he answered, with a queer, quiet sort of swagger in his tone and manner. "If anything ever did hurt, it's what I'm thinking of now; it might hurt less if I told you something about it."

"Then go on by all means. You may trust me to hold my tongue."

"My good fellow, why should you? Tell whom you like. It makes no difference. Nothing has made any difference for years. Besides, it's well enough known in the old country, though I've never spoken of it, drunk or sober, out here. I can't think why I should want to speak of it now—but I do."

He leant towards me and paused, admiring the white unbroken ash of his cigar, and half smiling. That half-smile was to me the saddest feature of a narrative of which it was the constant accompaniment. The tragic story which affected me so deeply seemed simply to interest the man who had brought the tragedy about. He told it in the fewest and the coolest words.

"One village and one woman—that's all. Deuce knows how many other women there were who could claim to come into the yarn, but I've forgotten them all but that one. There were plenty of villages, too, round about, including our own, but I'm only going to tell you of hers. Ours was not so much a village as a kingdom under the absolute rule of the most tyrannical old despot in this world—if he is in it still—I mean my father. He bullied and bossed the whole parish, including the parson, insulting the poor devil and threatening to have him suspended every other Sunday. He himself snarled out the lessons in church, and he made me learn texts by rote before I could read; for my father was one of those hard-bitten old saints who breed sinners like me the whole world over.

"But three miles from our village, which was in a constant simmer of discontent and suppressed rebellion, lay just the sweetest and most peaceful spot on earth, where it seems to me now that the sun was always shining. It was one long, old street of yellow walls and red tiles, and when you got to the end of it, there was the thatched church and the rectory, and the good old rector with his two hands stretched out to greet you, and hovering about him, to a certainty, the purest angel that ever wasted her love on a devil incarnate. I won't tell you the name of the village nor yet of the county. You'll be going back to the old dust one of these days, and you might run across my people. I don't want you to know it if you do. You may take your oath you won't hear of me from them; they've done their best to forget my existence. Oh, dear, yes, my name on the station books is as false as hell, like the rest of me. But I don't mind telling you her name. It was Edith, and I used to call her Edie. Jolly name, Edie, sweet and simple like the poor little thing herself. Rum thing, isn't it, how easily it still slips off my tongue?"

He stopped to smile me his strange impersonal smile, and to attend to his cigar. So far he had been holding it between finger and thumb, and admiring it as he talked.

"You will see how rum this is presently," he continued, with his eye on three fresh rings that were circling upward from his mouth. "We had been boy and girl together, but when we wanted to be man and wife, Edie's old father would not let us be engaged, because he knew of my blackguard ways. He did not give that as his reason. Edie was very young, a delicate slip of a girl, too, and it must have been a long engagement in any case. We were to remain friends, however. I think the dear old boy trusted to his girl to straighten me out first; if she couldn't, then nobody else could.

"But I was a hopeless case. The country-side rang with my sins long before I was sent down from Oxford; and went on ringing afterwards, louder and louder, when I settled in London and was nominally reading for the bar; but so long as I came down in time for prayers when I was at home, and went to hear our poor brow-beaten devil on Sundays, my father stopped his ears and shook his stick at those who tried to tell him of my misdeeds. I don't think he much cared what I did so long as he saw the soles of my boots at morning prayers. But my good old friend in the next parish was different. I can see him now, and the sorrow in his kind old face, when he forbade me the rectory once and for all. I felt that, too, and on my way home whom should I meet in the fields but Edith herself? So I made as clean a breast of everything as one could to a young girl. Young as she was though, you wouldn't believe how that girl sympathised and understood; and you won't believe this either, but her kindness fetched the tears to my eyes. She was a God's angel to me that summer day. I took her in my arms, little white feather that she was, and I vowed and vowed that I would keep straight for her sake even if I never saw her any more. And when I wouldn't touch her with my foul mouth she raised her pure lips—I can feel them now—and kissed my cheek of her own accord. She did indeed!"

His voice had become very sad and soft—so soft that I had to bend forward to catch some of the words—but there was a quiet bitter note in it that cut to the heart. And as he paused, and went on smoking, the queer sardonic smile came back to him. His cigar was now one half snowy ash, the other glossy brown leaf, and as he smoked a little red ring divided the two. He remarked afresh on the excellence of the ash before resuming his story in a lighter, louder tone that lasted him almost to the end.

"Now I'm going to tell you a very singular thing. I made my peace with the old rector, partly by letter, partly by Edie's intervention, and at Christmas-time I was to have her if she was still of her old mind; so at Christmas-time down I came from town with the engagement ring in my pocket. I knew that the girl would keep true to me through thick and thin, though I did hope that she had not heard of a certain matter which had got my name into the papers that autumn. Never mind what it was. My father had written very violently on the subject, but I had not heard a word from hers. So I hoped for the best. I was not as yet a fully reformed character, but I was about to become one. The night before I left town I never went to bed at all. It was my last orgy; but I was sober enough in the early morning to go to Covent Garden in my dress clothes, and to buy flowers to take down to Edie with the ring. I chose roses, because they were the most expensive at that time of year; and red ones, because the girl was naturally so pale.

Then I had a sleep in my chambers all the morning, and went down by an afternoon train.

"It was dark when I landed at the market-town where the dog-cart used to meet one. I hadn't ordered it this time, because I wasn't going straight home. I found it freezing down there, and I thought I would walk out to the rectory through the crisp night air, so as to arrive there fresh, for by now I felt the effects of the previous night. It was so very dark, however, that I bought a lantern and made them light it before I would set out on my three miles' walk. I remember going out of my way to a shop where I was not known. That market-town was our nearest one of any size, I had made it too hot to hold me before I was one-and-twenty, and it hadn't cooled down yet.

"The frost had followed a long spell of dirty weather, and the roads were fluted ribbons of frozen mud. My footsteps resounded merrily as I pushed into the darkness, the centre of a moving circle of light thrown upon the ground by my lantern. I shall never forget that walk. The box of flowers I carried in one hand, my lantern in the other, and for all my full hands I must needs keep feeling for the ring in my pocket, to make sure that I had it safe. And I felt as though my back was turned forever upon the town, and all that. We would be married without unnecessary delay, and we would live well outside London—either in the Thames Valley or among the Surrey Hills, I thought. At any price we would keep clear of the town; I would go in as late as possible in the mornings and return quite early in the afternoon. My old haunts should know me no more. With such a prospect and so many good resolutions to occupy my mind, the way seemed short enough, and I was glowing as much from my own thoughts as from the keen clean air when I swung open the rectory gate and walked briskly up the well-known drive; my heart was beating mountains high, for the dear old place had always been infinitely more homelike to me than my own home.

"The house struck me as being poorly lighted, but then I was purposely taking them by surprise. As I came up to it, my eyes mounted to Edie's bedroom window, and I was astonished to see it standing wide open to the bitter air. There was no light in the room either. The front door was opened by the rector himself. He seemed agitated at the sight of me; nor would he shake my hand, and I knew, then, that he had seen in the papers that which I hoped had escaped his notice. With a sinking heart I asked for Edie. The old man peered at me for a moment; then he answered that she was gone.

"'Gone away?'

"He nodded.

"'And when?'

"'This morning.'

"'And where to?' I asked, for you must see how disappointed I was.

"'Do not ask me,' he says. 'May God forgive you, for I, His minister, never can!' he sings out. And with that the door was shut in my face, and the key turned on the inside.

"God knows how long I remained standing like a fool on the gravel drive. The gravel must have been very soft before the hard frost which had set in that afternoon, for the light of my lantern struck down upon recent wheel-marks frozen stiff and clean. Instinctively I began to follow them. Edie had gone away, I was on her track. My thoughts were confused, but that was the drift of them. I followed the frozen wheel-marks out into the road, and on, on, on; it was not until I was following them in at the churchyard gate that my confusion fell from me, and left what soul there was in me naked to the freezing night air. Still my lantern fell upon the wheel-marks, and my feet followed them, until the light shone cold upon a narrow mound half hidden with white flowers. The fresh brown clay was already frozen as hard as the roads. I spent the night upon it, and should have frozen too, but I had started to run a hell of my own in my own heart. I'm running it still. When I crawled away before dawn there were some warm red roses among the cold white things. I was glad I had them. They're the one part of it I don't want ever to forget!"

His voice had sunk almost to a whisper, and for all the heat he gave such a shudder that the long ash was shaken at last from his cigar. I saw him gazing at the glowing end. All at once a fiery arc ran from his fingers through the air, and nearly the half of a prime Villar lay smouldering in the Riverina sun. I watched it meditatively, and the reed of heavy smoke ascending from it into the breathless air. I thought of the prostrate penitent upon the frozen grave. I marvelled at the refining spell which had bound the entire man for the last twenty minutes, utterly changing him. And I wondered how long that spell would survive its obvious source.

I wondered for one moment—with the soft, sad, gentlemanly voice still ringing in my ears—and for one moment only. The next, a bellow at my side drowned that voice forever; and Hell-fire Jim was himself again, screaming curses at his dog and his sheep, as one who realised that his reputation was at stake.

The dog was stretching itself awake in the slumbrous sunshine. The sheep were scattered down the gully as far as my eyes could see.

THE GOVERNESS AT GREENBUSH

I

The coach was before its time. As the owner of Greenbush drove into the township, the heavy, leather-hung, vermilion vehicle was the first object to meet his eyes. It was drawn up as usual in front of The Stockman's Rest, and its five horses were even yet slinking round to the yards, their traces flung across their smoking backs. The passengers had swarmed on the hotel verandah; but the squatter looked in vain for the flutter of a woman's skirt. What he took for one, from afar, resolved itself at shorter range into the horizontal moleskins of a stockman who was resting amid the passengers' feet, a living sign of the house. The squatter cocked a bushy eyebrow, but whistled softly in his beard next moment. He had seen the governess. She was not with the other passengers, nor had she already entered the hotel. She was shouldering her parasol, and otherwise holding herself like a little grenadier, alone but unabashed in the very centre of the broad bush street.

The buggy wheels made a sharp deep curve in the sand, the whip descended—the pair broke into a canter—the brake went down—and the man of fifty was shaking hands with the woman of twenty-five. They had met in Melbourne the week before, when Miss Winfrey had made an enviable impression and secured a coveted post. But Mr. Pickering had half forgotten her appearance in the interim, and taking another look at her now, he was quite charmed with his own judgment. The firm mouth and the decided chin were even firmer and more decided in the full glare of the Riverina sun than in the half-lights of the Melbourne hotel; and the expression of the grave grey eyes, which he had not forgotten, was, if possible, something franker and more downright than before. The face was not exactly pretty, but it had strength and ability. And strength especially was what was wanted in the station schoolroom.

"But what in the world, Miss Winfrey, are you doing here?" cried Mr. Pickering, after a rather closer scrutiny than was perhaps ideal. "I'm very sorry to be late, but why ever didn't you wait in the hotel?"

"There is a man dead-drunk on the verandah," returned the new governess, without mincing her words, and with a little flash in each steadfast eye.

"Well, but he wouldn't have hurt you!"

"He hurts me as it is, Mr. Pickering. I know nothing quite so sad as such sights, and I've seen more of them on my way up here than ever in my life before."

"Come, come, don't tell me it's worse than the old country," said the squatter, laughing, "or we shall fight all the way back! Now, will you jump up and come with me while I get your luggage; or shall we meet at the post-office over yonder on the other side?"

The girl looked round, following the direction of the pointed whip. "Yes, at the post-office, I think," and then she smiled. "It may seem an affectation, Mr. Pickering, but I'd really rather not go near the hotel again."

"Well, perhaps you're right. I'll be with you in five minutes, Miss Winfrey."

He flicked his horses: and in those five minutes the new governess made a friend for life in poor Miss Crisp the little old post-mistress. It was an unconscious conquest; indeed, she was thinking more of her employer than of anything she was saying; but this Miss Winfrey had a way of endearing herself to persons who liked being taken seriously, due perhaps to her own habit of taking herself very seriously indeed. Nevertheless, she was thinking of the squatter. He was a little rough, though less so, she thought, in his flannel shirt and wide-awake, than in the high collar and frock-coat which he had worn at their previous interview in Melbourne. On the whole she liked him well enough to wish to bring him to her way of looking at so distressing a spectacle as that of a drunken man. And it so happened that no sooner had she taken her seat beside him in the buggy than he returned of his own accord to the subject which was uppermost in her mind.

"It was one of my own men, Miss Winfrey."

"The man on the verandah?"

"Yes. They call him Cattle-station Bill. He looks after what we call the Cattle Station—an out-station of ours where there are nothing but sheep, by the way—on the other side of the township. He has a pretty lonely life over there. It's only natural he should knock down a cheque now and again."

The governess looked puzzled. "What does it mean—knocking down a cheque?"

"Mean? Well, we pay everything by cheque up here, d'you see? So when a man's put in his six months' work, say, he rolls up his swag and walks in for his cheque. Twenty-six pounds it would be for the six months, less a few shillings, we'll say, for tobacco. And most of 'em take their cheque to the nearest grog shanty and drink it up in three or four days."

Miss Winfrey shuddered.

"And then?"

"Then they come back to work for another six months."

"And you take them back?"

"I should think I did—when they're good men like Cattle-station Bill! It's nothing. He'll be back at his hut by the end of the week. That's an understood thing. Then in another few months he'll want another cheque. And so on, year in and year out."

Miss Winfrey made no remark, but she turned her head and looked back. And the recumbent moleskins were still a white daub on the hotel verandah, for it was hereabouts that Pickering had mistaken them for the young woman's skirt. She watched them out of sight, and then she sighed.

"It's terrible!"

"You'll get used to it."

"Never! It's too awful. One ought to do something. You must let me see what I can do, Mr. Pickering. The poor men! The poor men!"

Mr. Pickering was greatly amused. He never meddled with his men. Their morals were not his concern. In the matter of their cheques his sense of responsibility ended with his signature. The cheques might come back endorsed by a publican who, he knew, must have practically stolen them from his men's pockets. But he never meddled with that publican.

It was none of his business; but to find a little bit of a governess half inclined to make it *her* business was a most original experience, and it was to Pickering's credit that he was able to treat the matter in a spirit of pure good-humour.

"I rather think our brats will take you all your time," said he, laughing heartily. "Still, I'll let you know next time Bill comes in for a cheque, and you shall talk to him like a mother. He's a very good-looking young fellow, I may tell you that!"

Miss Winfrey was about to answer, quite seriously, that she would be only too glad of an opportunity of speaking to the poor man; but the last remark made the rest, from her point of view, unanswerable. Moreover, it happened to hurt, and for a reason that need be no secret. Her own romance was over. She had no desire for another. That one had left her rather a solemn young woman with, however, a perfectly sincere desire to do some good in the world, to undo some of the evil.

The squatter repeated this conversation to his wife, who had not, however, his own good-nature. "I don't see what business it was of Miss Winfrey's," remarked Mrs. Pickering, who had not been with her husband when he selected the governess. "It was quite a presumption on her part to enter into such a discussion, and I should have let her know it had I been there.

But I am afraid she is inclined to presume, James. Those remarks of hers about poetry were hardly the thing for her first meal at our table. Did you hear her correct me when I mentioned Lewis William Morris? She said they were two separate men!"

"She probably knew what she was talking about. I didn't go and engage a fool, my dear."

"It was a piece of impudence," said Mrs. Pickering hotly; "and after what you have told me now, James, I can't say I feel too favourably impressed with Miss Winfrey."

"Then I'm very sorry I told you anything," retorted Pickering with reflected warmth. "The girl's all right; but you always were ready to take a prejudice against anybody. Just you wait a bit! That girl's a character. I'll wager she makes your youngsters mind her as they've never minded anybody in their lives!"

The lady sighed; she had poor health and an irritable, weak nature; and her "youngsters" had certainly never "minded" their mother. She took her husband's advice; she waited; and such was the order that presently obtained among her band of little rebels, and so great and novel the relief and rest which crept into her own daily life, that for many weeks—in fact, until the novelty wore off—Miss Winfrey could do no wrong, and the children's mother had not words good enough for their new governess.

The children themselves were somewhat slower to embrace this optimistic view. They came to it at last, but only by the steep and stony path of personal defeat and humiliation. Miss Winfrey had the wit to avoid the one irretrievable mistake on the part of all such as would govern as well as teach. She never tried for an immediate popularity with her pupils, which she felt would be purchased at the price of all future influence and power. On the contrary, she was content to be hated for weeks and feared for months; but the fear gradually subsided in respect; and presently respect was joined by love. Now, love is the teacher's final triumph. And little Miss Winfrey won hers in the face of sufficiently formidable odds.

It was a case of four to one. Three of the four were young men, however, with whom the young woman who is worth her salt well knows how to deal. These young men were employed upon the station, and they had petted and spoilt the children pretty persistently hitherto. It had been their favourite relaxation after the day's work in the saddle or at the drafting yards. Miss Winfrey took to playing their accompaniments as they had never been played before, and very soon it was tacitly agreed among them that the good-will of the governess was a better thing than the adoration of her class. So the three gave very little trouble after all; but the fourth made up for their defection; and the fourth knew better how to fight a woman.

She was one herself.

Millicent Pickering was the children's half-sister, the only child of her father's first marriage. She was a sallow, weedy, and yet attractive-looking girl of nineteen, with some very palpable faults, which, however, were redeemed by the saving merit of a superlatively good temper. She loved a joke, and her idea of one was quite different from that of Miss Winfrey, who, to be sure, was not a little deficient in this very respect. Millicent found her sense of humour best satisfied by the enormities of her little brothers and sisters. She rallied them openly upon the punishments inflicted by their governess; she was in notorious and demoralising sympathy with the young offenders. Out of school she encouraged them in every branch of wickedness; and, for an obvious reason, was ever the first to lead them into temptations which now ended in disgrace. She was, of course, herself the greatest child of them all; and at last Miss Winfrey told her so in as many words. She would have spoken earlier, but that she feared to jeopardise her influence by risking a defeat. But when the great girl took to interrupting the very lesson with her overgrown buffooneries, in the visible vicinity of the open schoolroom door, the time was come to beat or be beaten once and for all.

"Come in, Miss Pickering," said the governess suavely, though her heart was throbbing. "I think I should have the opportunity of laughing too."

The girl strode in, and the laughter rose louder than before. But, however excruciatingly funny her antics might have been outside, they were not continued within.

"Well?" said Miss Winfrey at length.

"Well?" retorted Millicent with mere sauce.

"You great baby!" cried the governess, with a flush and a flash that came like lightning. "You deserve to have your hair taken down, and be put back into short dresses and a pinafore!"

"And sent to you?"

"And sent to me."

"Right you are! I'll come this afternoon."

And she did. When school began again, at three o'clock, Millicent led the way, with her hair down and her dress up, and in her hands the largest slate she could find; and on her face a kind of determined docility, exquisitely humorous to the expectant young eyes behind the desks. But Millicent had reckoned without her brains, and that in more senses than one. She was an exceedingly backward young person; she had never been properly taught, and no one knew this better than the little governess. First in one simple subject, then in another, the ignorance of the girl was mercilessly exposed; first by one child, then by another, she was corrected and enlightened on some elementary point; and finally, when they all stood up and took places, Miss Millicent sank to the bottom of the class in five minutes. The absurd figure that she cut there, however, with the next child no higher than her waist, quite failed to appeal to her usually ready sense of humour; seeing which, Miss Winfrey incontinently dismissed the class; but Millicent remained behind.

"I give you best," said she, holding out a large hand with a rather laboured smile. "Let's be friends."

"I have always wanted to," said the victor, with a suspicious catch in her voice. Next moment she burst into a flood of tears. And that war was won.

Millicent had long needed such a friend; but this new influence was a better thing for her than any one ever knew. She happened to be fond of somebody who was very fond of her; and having one of those impulsive natures which fly from one extreme to the other, she told Miss Winfrey that very night all about it. And Miss Winfrey advised. And on the next monthly visitation of a certain rabbit inspector to Greenbush Station the light-hearted Millicent succeeded in reconciling her sporting spirit to what she termed the "dry-hash" of a serious engagement.

But not for long. As the more solemn side of the matter came home to her, the light heart grew heavy with vague alarms, and so bitterly did the young girl resent her entirely natural apprehensions, that cause and effect became confounded in her soul, now calling, as she thought, for its surrendered freedom. Her depression was terrible, and yet more terrible her disappointment in herself. She could not be in love, or, if she were, then love was not what it was painted by all the poets whose works the sympathetic Miss Winfrey now put into her hands. Thus the first month passed. Then the man came again, and in his presence her doubt lay low in her heart; but when he was gone it rose up blacker than before, and the girl went near to madness with keeping it to herself. It was only the agony of an ignorant young egoism in the twilight state of the betrothed, looking backward with regret for yesterday's freedom, instead of forward faithfully to a larger life. But this never struck her until she brought her broodings to her friend Miss Winfrey, when one flesh could endure them no longer.

Miss Winfrey was surprised. She had not suspected so much soul in such a setting. She was also sorry, for she liked the man. He had kind eyes and simple ways, and yet some unmistakable signs of the sort of strength which appealed to the governess and would be good for Milly. And lastly, Miss Winfrey was strangely touched: for here was her own case over again.

The girl said that she could never marry him, that there was no love in her for any man, that she must break off the engagement instantly and for all time; the governess had said the same thing at her age, and had repented it ever since. The governess turned down the lamp, for it was late at night in the schoolroom, and she told the girl her own story. This had more weight than a hundred arguments. Half-way through, Millicent took Miss Winfrey's hand and held it to the end; at the very end she kissed the governess and made her a promise.

"Thank you, dear," said Miss Winfrey, kissing Milly. "That was all I wanted you to say. Only try for a time to think less of yourself and more of him! Then all will be well; and you may forget my contemptible little story. You're the first to whom I've ever told it as it really was."

"And you never saw him again?"

"Not from that day to this."

"But you may, dear Miss Winfrey. You may!"

"It isn't likely," said the governess, turning up the lamp. "I came out here to—forget. He is a full-blown doctor by now, and no doubt happily married."

"Never!" cried Millicent.

"Long ago," laughed Miss Winfrey. "The worse they take it at the time the sooner they marry. That is—men; and you can't alter them."

"I don't believe it's every man," said the young girl stoutly. "I don't even believe it's—yours."

Miss Winfrey bent her head to hide her eyes. "Sometimes," she whispered, "I don't believe so either."

"And if—you met—and all was right?"

The governess got to her feet. Her face was lifted, and the tears transfigured it. It was white and shining like the angel-faces in a little child's dream. And her lips trembled with the trembling words: "I should ask him to forgive me for the wrong I did him. I would humiliate myself as I humiliated him. It would be my pride. He might not care; but he should know that I had—all along!"

II

Miss Winfrey grew very fond of her schoolroom. There, as the young men told her, she was "her own boss," with a piano, though a poor one, all to herself; and a desk, the rather clumsy handiwork of the eldest boy, yet her very own, and full of her own things. She took an old maid's delight in orderly arrangement, and, for that matter, was not loath to own, with her most serious air, that she quite intended to be an old maid. But what she liked best about the schoolroom was its fundamental privacy. It formed a detached building, and had formerly been the station store. The old dining-room was the present store, which was entered by the "white verandah," so known in contradistinction to the deep, trellised shelter—which, however, Mrs. Pickering insisted on calling the "piazza"—belonging to a later building. The white verandah was narrow and bald by comparison. But the young men still burnt their evening incense upon it, while Millicent and the governess preferred it at all hours of the day. It was just opposite the schoolroom, for one thing; for another, Mrs. Pickering but seldom set foot on the white verandah, and the peevish lady was not a popular character in the homestead of which she was mistress.

She no longer approved of the new governess. Miss Winfrey's singular success with the children had been quite sufficient to alienate their mother's sympathies, or rather to revive her prejudices. Her feeling in the matter was not, perhaps, altogether inhuman. It is difficult to appreciate the expert manipulation of material upon which we ourselves have tried an ineffectual hand. It is odious to see another win through sheer discipline to a popularity which all one's own indulgence has failed to secure. These experiences were Mrs. Pickering's just deserts, but that did not lessen their sting. The lady became not unnaturally jealous of her children's friend, whose society they now obviously preferred to her own. With former governesses not a day had passed without one child or another coming to its mother with some whining tale. There were no such complaints now; but the mother missed them as she would have missed so many habitual caresses; for it made her feel that she was no longer everything to her children. It is easier to understand her feelings than to forgive their expression. She took to snubbing the governess in the pupils' presence. It is true that, as the young men said, Mrs. Pickering did not "get much change" out of little Miss Winfrey. The girl was well qualified to take care of herself. But she was more sensitive than she cared to show. Her whole soul shrank from the small contentions which were forced upon her; they hurt her equally whether she won or she lost. Still it was less horrid to win, and one little victory gave the governess distinct satisfaction.

Mrs. Pickering took it into her head that the children were worked too hard. So one afternoon she walked into the schoolroom and told them all that they might go—nearly an hour before the time. But not a child stirred.

"You may all run away," repeated their mother. "Do you hear me? Then why don't you move?"

The eldest boy shuffled awkwardly in his place. "Please, mother, it's poetry-hour, and we only have it once a week."

Mrs. Pickering, relying on the little ones, now called for a show of hands. But the very infants were against her; and she left the room with a bitter glance at the silent governess, who after a moment's consideration dismissed the class herself. Meantime the irate lady had gone straight to her husband.

"Miss Winfrey is becoming unendurable," she told him in the tone of personal reproach which had already made the unlucky squatter curse his choice of a governess. "The poor children are positively frightened to death of her! I went in to let them out of school; no one but an inhuman monster would keep them in on an afternoon like this; and actually, not one of them dared to move without Miss Winfrey's permission! Harry muttered something to the effect that they would rather finish the lesson, and the rest sat still, but you may be sure they knew it was either that or being punished afterwards. How I hate such severities! As for that woman herself, she sat like a mule without saying anything. Ah! I see she's thought better of it, and let them out herself; to show that her authority's superior to mine, I suppose! Really, that's the last straw!"

Pickering met his wife judiciously, but not by any means half-way. He knew what she meant; he was not himself entirely enamoured of Miss Winfrey. She had spoken to him about the boys seeing too much of the men out mustering on Saturdays, a point on which the father deemed himself the best judge. She had too many opinions of her own; but when all was said, she was an admirable governess. He dwelt upon the general improvement in the children under Miss Winfrey. He had the sense to ignore their very evident affection for that martinet. Another change might be a very good thing in a few months' time, but at present it would be a thousand pities. Christmas was coming on. It would be very easy to let Miss Winfrey see that her daily supervision was not required during the holidays. She could have the time to herself.

She did have the time to herself, and a very poor time it was. The parents gave out that they intended to see something of their young people while they had the chance. And to broaden the hint, as if that were necessary, they studiously refrained from inviting Miss Winfrey to join in the daily entertainment. Now it was a family visit to a neighbouring station, with four horses in the big trap; now a picnic in the scrub, now impromptu races on the township course. The governess spent the days in her own schoolroom, with little intervals on the white verandah. Millicent's rabbit inspector was at Greenbush, so Miss Winfrey saw nothing of Millicent either. All was now well between those two: on the day he went, she rode with him to the boundary fence, and then joined the picnic party in the Forest Paddock.

"Where's Miss Winfrey?" cried the girl, from her saddle, as she cantered up to the little group about the crackling fire.

The children looked unhappy.

"She's at home," said Harry.

Millicent asked why.

"Because it's holidays," answered Mrs. Pickering, looking up from the basket which she was unpacking. "Because we've come out to enjoy ourselves."

Millicent ran over the ring of little wistful faces, and a soft laugh curled her lips. She could hear her father gathering branches in the scrub, and talking to the only young man who had not gone away for his holidays. She wondered whether she should dismount at all; her heart went out to her friend all alone at the homestead; she, too, had neglected her these last few days.

"When did Miss Winfrey spoil a day's enjoyment?" the girl demanded. "She would have added to it."

"You may think so. I chose not to risk it."

"But surely you gave her a chance of coming?"

"Not I, indeed! The children see quite enough of their governess in school. Harry, darling, there's the water boiling at last."

But Millicent was boiling too. "That settles it," she exclaimed with a quick flush. "Good-bye, all of you!" And she was gone at a hand-gallop.

Little love was to lose between the girl and her step-mother. Millicent was rather glad than otherwise to turn her back upon a party which did not include the one daily companion who was now entirely congenial to her, while if anybody could fill at all the gaping blank left by her lover's departure, it was Miss Winfrey, who was always so sympathetic, so understanding. To that same sympathy the young girl felt that she owed her present abiding and increasing happiness, and again her heart went out to the counsellor who had known no such counsel in her own black hour of doubt and trepidation. Otherwise—and Milly sighed. She knew the whole story now. Her friend had spoken of it a second and a third time, and the speaking had seemed to do her good. It was five years ago. The young man had been a medical student then. And now his penitent false love could see him only as a thriving doctor—and a married man.

"I would give anything to find him," thought the girl who was happy, as she stooped to open the home-paddock gate. "I know—something tells me—that he is true!"

She cantered to the homestead, standing high and hot on its ridge of sand, with only a few dry pines sprouting out of the yard. The year was burning itself out in a succession of torrid days, of which this was the worst hitherto. The sky was prodigiously, ridiculously blue, with never a flake of cloud from rim to rim. The wind came from the north as from an open oven. And Millicent's dog was running under the very girths of her horse, whose noon-day shadow she could not see.

She watered both animals at the tank, and then rode on to the horse-yard; but, ere she reached it, was much struck by the sound of a sweet voice singing in the distance. It seemed a queer thing, but the young woman from England was standing the Riverina summer far better than those who had been born there. She could sit and sing on a day like this!

On her way on foot from the horse-yard to the schoolroom Millicent stood on her shadow to listen to the song. The governess sang very seldom; she liked better to play accompaniments for the young men, though she had a charming, trained voice of her own. Millicent had never heard her use it, as she was doing now, without a known soul within earshot save the Chinaman in the kitchen.

The heat of the sand struck through the young girl's boots. Yet still she stood, her head bent, and at last caught a few of the words:

"... in the lime-tree,
The wind is floating through:

And oh! the night, my darling, is sighing—
Sighing for you, for you."

A verse was finished. Millicent crept nearer. She had never heard such tender singing. Three or four simple bars and it began again:

"O think not I can forget you;
I could not though I would;

I see you in all around me,
The stream, the night, the wood;

The flowers that slumber so gently,
The stars above the blue.

Oh! heaven itself, my darling, is praying—
Praying for you, for you."

The voice sank very low, its pathos was infinite, yet the listener heard every word. There were no more. Millicent dried her eyes, and went tripping over her habit through the open schoolroom door. There sat the governess, with wrung face and grey eyes all intensity.

"My dear, it was divine!"

"You heard! I'm sorry."

"But why?"

"I never sing that song."

"Why, again?"

The fixed eyes fell. "It was—his favourite.... The music is better than the words, I think; don't you? But then the words are a translation."

Complete change of tone forbade further questioning. But once more the younger girl felt horribly discontented with her own really adequate affection for the honest rabbit inspector. It seemed such a little thing beside the passion of her friend.

Not long after this Millicent was reclining on a deck-chair under shelter of the white verandah. The heat was still intense, and she was nearly asleep. It was a Saturday afternoon, the children were abroad in the paddocks, but their governess was in her own schoolroom, for once as enervated as Millicent herself, who could just see the hem of her frock through the open door.

Millicent had closed her eyes. A spur clinked on the verandah, but she was too lazy to lift a lid. A voice said, "Is Mr. Pickering about, please, miss?" with a good accent, but in a curious hang-dog tone. She answered, "You'll find him in the store," without troubling to see which of the men it was. Then came sleep ... then her father, shaking her softly, and whispering in her ear.

"It's Cattle-station Bill," he said. "Wants another cheque—hasn't had one since the day Miss Winfrey came. Where is she, Milly? She seemed to think she'd like to try her hand at reforming our Bill, and now's her chance. He's only gone five months this time!"

"Miss Winfrey's in the schoolroom," replied Milly drowsily. "She won't thank you for disturbing her any more than I do."

Pickering stepped down into the sand and crossed over to the schoolroom, dragging a shadow like a felled pine. The man was meanwhile in the store, where presently his master rejoined him in fits of soft and secret laughter. And Millicent rubbed her eyes, because her nap had been ruined, and bent them upon the schoolroom door, in which the governess now stood reading a book.

The spurs clinked again on the verandah, the book dropped over the way, the governess disappeared from view; and Millicent glanced from the empty door to the wearer of the spurs. He was a handsome young fellow, with blue-black hair and moustache, and a certain indefinable distinction of which his rough clothes could not rid him. But his eyes were turned sullenly to earth, and as he snatched his horse's reins from the hook on the verandah-post with his right hand, his left crumpled up his cheque and rammed it into his pocket. And a wild suspicion flashed across Millicent at that moment, to be confirmed the next.

"Last night the nightingale woke me,"

sang the voice in the schoolroom;

"Last night, when all was still,
It sang in the golden moonlight,
From out the woodland hill."

Milly had not taken her eyes from the sullen handsome stockman standing almost at her feet. His left hand was still in his pocket; his right had the reins, but was still outstretched in front of him—as though petrified—while a white, scared face turned this way and that with the perspiration welling from every pore. Yet the smooth agony of the song went on without a tremor....

"And oh! the bird, my darling, was singing—
Singing of you, of you."

As the verse ended, the man shivered from head to foot, then flung himself into the saddle, and Millicent watched him ride headlong towards the home-paddock gate. She lost sight of him, however, long before he reached it, and then she knew that Miss Winfrey was still singing her song in a loud, clear voice. Could she be mistaken? It was a sufficiently wild idea. Could it be nothing but coincidence after all? Again she caught the words:

"I think of you in the daytime,
I dream of you by night,

I wake, and would you were here, love,
And tears are blinding my sight.

I hear a low breath in the lime-tree——"

The sweet air, the tender words, snapped short together. Millicent sprang
from her deck-chair, heard a fall as she ran, and found the governess in a
swoon upon the schoolroom floor.

III

"What did he do?"

They were the first faint words that fell from the bloodless lips, and
Millicent was much too thankful to think twice of their meaning. Besides,
she had things to ask the governess. How was she now? Was her head too
low? Had she hurt herself as she fell?

"What did he do?" repeated the faint voice a little less faintly.

"Dear, I will tell you in a minute——"

"Tell me now. What did he do? Did he—remember?"

Millicent did her best to describe the effect of the song upon the man. She
omitted nothing.

The governess gave a great sigh. "Thank God!" she said. "There was no
time to think. It was all on the spur of the moment. But I knew that you
were there, that you'd see. And you saw all that; it was all there for you to
see!" She closed her eyes, and her lips moved in further thanksgiving.

"Dear, I saw—his soul," said Milly timidly; "it is not dead. I saw more—I
saw his love!"

The fair head shook.

"No; that must be dead."

"Then why should it move him so? Why should he mind? What could the
song be to him, if you were nothing? Dear, you are everything—still!"

The fair head shook again, and more decidedly.

"It's impossible. But I may *do* something. I have brought him to this, and
I'll bring him back from it, with God's help!"

And as she stood up suddenly, to her last inch, Milicent again beheld the white, keen face touched for an instant with all the radiant exaltation of the Angelic Hosts.

"I might have known it," continued Miss Winfrey, in a calmer, more contemplative tone. "I knew him; I might have guessed the rest. Such troubles come and go with the ordinary young man, but Wilfrid was never that. His name is Wilfrid Ferrers, Milly—your Cattle-station Bill! As I have told you, his father was a country clergyman; and clergymen's sons are always the worst. Willie had been rather wild before I knew him; he used to tell me all about it, for he was the most open-hearted boy in all the world, and could keep nothing to himself. If he could, he wouldn't; for sail under his true colours he must, he used to say, even if they were the black flag. But they weren't. His wildness was one-half high spirits, and the other half good-nature. But it showed the man. He had once—I almost smile when I remember how he was once before the magistrates for some reckless boyish folly at the hospital! He would stick at nothing; but he used to say that I could do what I liked with him, make what I would of him. And what have I made?" cried the unhappy girl, in a relapse as sudden as her resolve. "A broken heart—a broken life!" She sank down at one of the desks, threw her arms upon the slope, and wept passionately. And yet again she was up, rapping the desk with her knuckles as she would in school, and staring masterfully at Millicent, out of her streaming eyes.

"What am I saying? What I have done, I can undo; what I have ruined, I can redeem. This is no coincidence, Milly; never tell me that! It is God's plan. He in His mercy means me to repair my wrong. He has given me this chance.... I am going to my own room, Milly. I want you to leave me alone, dear. I want to thank Him on my knees. And then—and then—I may be shown how to act!"

The livelong afternoon she spent alone with her emergency. The homestead was very quiet. The young men were still away. The first sounds that penetrated to Miss Winfrey's room were the merry voices of the returning children. But by this time the governess had made up her mind. She now arose, and going forth in her right mind, found Millicent hovering near the door. The girls linked arms, and sauntered in the home-paddock till dinner-time.

"Here are his tracks," cried Millicent, halting in excitement. "His galloping tracks!"

The governess had not the bush girl's eye for a trail. To her, one hoof-mark was like another, and they honeycombed the rude soft road in millions. But she followed Milly's finger with thoughtful eyes, and presently she put a question.

"How far is it to the cattle station?"

"Fourteen miles."

"Five to the township, and——"

"Nine beyond. You turn to the left, and take the bridle-path to the right. Then you come to a gate. Then you cross a five-mile paddock; and it's half-way across the next one, close to the left-hand fence."

"Thank you. I shall go and see him."

"When he gets back?"

"Gets back! Where from?"

"The township," said Milly reluctantly.

"Did he look to you as though he were going there?"

"I—I certainly thought so; but I daresay I was wrong. I'm sure I was!" cried Milly.

"I wish I were sure," said Miss Winfrey with a sigh. "Yes, dear," she added, "I shall wait until he gets back."

A voice said close behind them that the dinner was getting cold. The voice was Mrs. Pickering's. In the sand they had heard no step; both girls changed colour, and in Mrs. Pickering's eye there was a curious light. But she had never been more civil to Miss Winfrey than at dinner that night; and after dinner she clamoured for a song. This was almost unprecedented. And the song she wanted was the song which she had heard in the distance that afternoon. But the governess made her excuses, and went early to her own room.

An hour later there was a tentative, light knock at Miss Winfrey's door—and no answer. Mrs. Pickering knocked again and louder. She carried a lighted candle; her hand trembled, and the hot grease spattered the floor. There was still no answer, so the lady tried the door. It was unlocked. She walked in. "I thought so!" muttered Mrs. Pickering, in a triumphant tone. She passed her candle over the untouched bed; she poked it into the empty corner; and it was some minutes before she could bring herself to quit the deserted room that filled her with so shrewd a sense of personal satisfaction.

That satisfaction was only too well founded. It was then just eleven, and at that very minute the indomitable Miss Winfrey was tramping into view of the township lights. They were few enough at such an hour. The Stockman's Rest, however, was both alight and alive, and midnight oil was burning in the post-office over the way. Miss Winfrey hesitated, bent her steps towards the post-office, hesitated again, and finally marched straight across to the hotel. The verandah was empty. She did not set foot on it. She could see into the bar.... She did not think he was there.... If only she could be sure!

In the end a groundless panic overcame her, and to the post-office she fled pell-mell. There, however, she recovered herself sufficiently to recall the pretext with which she had come prepared, and to drop a sham missive in the box before knocking.

It was the post-mistress herself who unlocked the door, who stood on the threshold with a lamp held high, her kind face wrinkled with surprise and concern.

"Why—bless the lot of us!—it's never Miss Winfrey?"

"It is," said the governess, with a wan smile and a hand on her heart. "Will you let me sit down, and—not ask what brings me?"

Miss Crisp pushed her pale visitor into a chair.

"Perhaps I know," said she slyly. "That letterbox makes a noise!"

"Oh, to be so deceitful!" moaned Miss Winfrey, red with shame.

"Tut!" said her ready dupe; "I only call it venturesome. I know *I* shouldn't like to have all my letters seen when they make up the station mail-bag, though I don't know the thing that would bring me all this way on foot at this time of night. However, that's your business, my dear, and you shall have a cup of tea before I let you go again."

The two had often foregathered since the day of Miss Winfrey's arrival, and the fact made her feel meaner than ever now. Yet she could not bring herself to tell the post-mistress everything, and it was either that or the small deceit which she was practising. Consciously or unconsciously Miss Crisp must help her. They took the same strong view of the dreadful system of knocking down cheques; the governess proceeded to turn this to account. She referred to their first meeting, and as casually as possible to Cattle-station Bill, saying the poor man had been in for another cheque that afternoon.

"Indeed?" said Miss Crisp, seating herself till the kettle should boil. "He didn't get one, did he?"

"He did. That's just it. What makes you think he did not?"

"He never stopped on his way back."

"Not—opposite?"

"No."

The girl's heart danced.

"Are you positive?"

"Quite. He's back at his hut, for I saw him go—galloping like a mad thing!"

"What time was that?"

"Between four and five."

The governess was too clever to drop the subject suddenly. She said she had made sure the poor man's cheque had gone the same way as the last, and so obtained a second assurance that as yet, at all events, it had not. Miss Crisp of the post-office saw most of what went on in the township; the rest was sure to reach her ears. So Miss Winfrey acted her part to the last, and took leave of her little old friend with a guilty and a penitent heart. But go on she must; it was too late to turn back, too late to think.

She made an elaborate *détour*, and struck the main road once more considerably to the left of the township. That amounted to the same thing as turning to the left through the township street. She now stood still to rehearse the remainder of Milly's directions, which she had by heart. She was to take the bridle-path to the right, which would bring her to a gate; she was then to cross a five-mile paddock; and—that was enough for the present.

The bridle-path was easily found. It brought her to the gate without let or panic. But by this time the girl had walked many miles and her feet were very sore. So she perched herself upon the gate, and watched an attenuated moon float clear of the inhospitable sandhills, and sail like a silver gondola on a sombre sea. But as the ache left her feet, it crept into her heart with all the paralysing wonder as to what she should say and do when at last she found her poor love. And immediately she jumped down and continued her tramp; for she was obliged to do what she was doing; only it was easier to walk, than to look, ahead.

The thin moon was much higher when its wan rays shone once more upon the wires of a fence running right and left into the purple walls of the night. There were no trees now. The vague immensity of the plains was terrifying to the imaginative girl, who had felt for some time as if she were walking by a miracle upon a lonely sea: a miracle that might end any moment: a sea that supported her on sufferance capriciously. But with the fence and the gate came saner thought, and a clear sight of the true occasion for fear and trembling. She was now within two or three miles of the hut. What was she to do when she got there? She did not know, she would not think. She would get there first, and leave the rest to that fate which had urged her so far.

She went through this gate without resting; she was no longer conscious of bodily pains. She followed up the fence on the left, according to Milly's directions, walking at the top of her speed for half an hour. Then all at once she trembled and stood still: there was the hut. It was as though it had risen out of the ground, so sudden was the sight of it, standing against the fence, one end towards her, scarce a hundred yards from where she was. She got no farther just then; the courage of her act forsook her at the last. She had no more strength of heart or limb, and she sank to the ground with a single sob. The slip of a moon was sickening in a sallow sky when the girl stood up next.

The dawn put new life in her will. She would wait till sunrise before she made a sound. Meanwhile, if the hut door was open, she would perhaps peep in. The door was open; there was a faint light within; she could see it through the interstices of the logs as she approached; it fell also in a sickly, flickering beam upon the sand without. And after a little, she did peep in: to see a "slush-lamp" burning on the table, and, in the wretched light of it, the figure of a man, with his bare arms and hidden face upon the table too. He seemed asleep; he might have been dead.

"Wilfrid!"

He was alive. The white face flashed upon her. The wild eyes started and stared. Then slowly, stiffly, unsteadily, he rose, he towered.

"So it was you I heard—singing that song!"

"Yes, Wilfrid."

"It is unbelievable. I've dreamt it often enough, but——yes, it's you! So you've found me out!"

"By the merest accident. I had no idea of it until to-day."

She was terrified at his eyes; they hungered, and were yet instinct with scorn. He stuck his spurred foot upon the box which had been his seat, and leaned forward, looking at her, his brown arms folded across his knee.

"And now?" he said.

She took one step, and laid her warm hands upon his arms, and looked up at him with flaming face, with quivering lips, with streaming eyes. "And now," she whispered, "I am ready to undo the past——"

"Indeed!"

"To make amends—to keep my broken word!"

He looked at her a moment longer, and his look was very soft. He had heard her singing, but neither the song nor the voice had done more than remind him of her. And yet the mere reminder had carried him through the township with a live cheque in his pocket—had kept him sitting up all night with his false love's image once more unveiled in his heart. Here by a miracle was his love herself; she loved him now—now that she had made him unworthy of her love! Little wonder that he looked softly at her for a moment more; and the next, still less wonder that he flung those hot hands from him, and kicked the box from under his foot, and recoiled with a mocking laugh from the love that had come too late.

"Keep what you like," he cried out with a brutal bitterness; "only keep your pity to yourself! You should require it. I don't."

And the girl was still staring at him, in a dumb agony, an exquisite torture, when the smack of a riding-whip resounded on the corrugated roof, and the eyes of both flew to the door.

IV

A horse's mane and withers, rubbed by the rider's beard as he stooped to peer into the hut, deepened the grey dusk within and made the lamp burn brighter. Then came the squatter's voice, in tremulous, forced tones, as of a man who can ill trust himself to speak.

"And so, Miss Winfrey, you are here!"

The governess came close to the threshold and faced her employer squarely, though without a word. Then her song had awakened a memory, but nothing more! So ran her thoughts.

"Your explanation, Miss Winfrey?"

"We knew each other years ago." And she waved with her hand towards the man who would not stand beside her in her shame.

"May I ask when you found that out?"

"Yesterday afternoon."

"Ah, when he came in for his cheque. I may tell you that I saw something of it from the store; and my wife happened to overhear some more when she went to fetch you and my daughter in to dinner."

"That was very clever of Mrs. Pickering."

"It was an accident; she couldn't help hearing."

"I daresay!" cried the governess, taking fire at the first spark. "But I shall tell her what I think of such accidents when I see her again!"

There was no immediate answer. And the girl took a cold alarm; for a soft meaning laugh came through the door; and either behind her, or in her imagination, there was an echo which cut her to the quick.

"May I ask," said Mr. Pickering, "when you expect to see my wife again?"

"Never!" said the girl, as though she had known that all along; but she had not thought of it before, and the thing stunned her even as she spoke.

"Never," repeated the squatter, with immense solemnity. "You've treated her very badly, Miss Winfrey; she feels it very much. You might at least have consulted her before going to such a length as this. A length which has nothing to do with me, mark you; but I must say it is one of the most scandalous things I ever heard of in all my life. I'm sorry to speak so strongly. I'm sorry to lose you for the children; but you must see that you're no longer quite the sort of person we want for them. You will find your boxes on the coach which leaves the township this evening, and your cheque——"

"Stop!" said a hoarse voice fiercely. At the same moment Miss Winfrey was forced to one side, and Wilfrid Ferrers filled her place: she had never admired him so much as now, with his doubled fists, and his rough dress, and the cold dawn shining on his haggard face. "You've said quite enough," he continued; "now it's my turn, Mr. Pickering. Miss Winfrey hasn't been at the hut ten minutes. She came because we were old friends, to try to make me the man I was when she knew me before. Unfortunately it's a bit too late; but she wasn't to know that, and she's done no wrong. Now apologise—or settle it with me!" and he laid hold of the bridle.

"You may let go those reins," replied Pickering. "I'm not frightened of you, though you have the better of me by twenty years. But I think you're on the right side in a more important respect than that; and if I've done Miss Winfrey an injustice, I hope I'm man enough to apologise in my own way." He slid from his horse, and walked into the hut with his wide-awake in one hand, and the other outstretched. "I beg your pardon," he said.

"I don't blame you," she replied.

He kept her hand kindly.

"Perhaps we shall meet again, Miss Winfrey. I hope so. I don't know how it stands between you two, but I can give a guess. You're a good girl; and we've always known what Bill was underneath. Good luck to you both! I shall send another man out here to-night."

The girl stood still and heard him ride away. The soft words stung worse than the harsh, she scarcely knew why. She was bewildered and aching in heart and body and brain. On some point she should have enlightened Mr. Pickering, but she had let it pass, and now what was it?

Ferrers had accompanied the squatter outside; had seen him start; and now he was standing in front of her with eyes that seemed to speak to her out of the past.

"Two men have insulted you this morning," he was saying. "One has apologised; it is the other's turn now. Forgive me——Lena!"

It was his old voice. The tears rushed to her eyes, and she stepped out blindly for the door. "I have nothing to forgive!" she cried. "Let me go. Only let me go!"

"Go where?"

"To the township—anywhere! I should have told Mr. Pickering. Call him back!—Ah, he's so far away already! What am I to do? What am I to do?"

Ferrers pushed the wooden box into the doorway where she stood leaning heavily against the jamb. "Sit down on that," said he, "while I brew you some tea. You're tired to death. Time enough to think of things after."

The girl sat down, and for a while she cried gently to herself. Her physical fatigue was enormous, rendering her perfectly helpless for the time being, with a helplessness which she resented more bitterly than the incomparable mental torments of the situation. These she deserved. If only she could get away, and turn this bitter page before it drove her mad! If only she could creep away, and close her eyes for hours or for ever! Surely this was the refinement of her punishment, that the flesh, which had stood her in too good stead hitherto, should fail her utterly in her supreme need!

The red sun burst out of the plains, as it were under her very eyes—blinding them. Miss Winfrey would not look round. She heard matches struck, sticks crackling, and later, the "billy" bubbling on the fire. She knew when the "slush-lamp" was extinguished; her sense of smell informed her of the fact. She heard a chop frizzling at the fire, the cutting of the damper on the table; but not until Ferrers touched her on the shoulder, telling her that breakfast was ready, would she turn her head or speak a word. The touch made her quiver to the core. He apologised, explaining that he had spoken thrice. Then they sat down; and the girl ate ravenously; but Ferrers did little but make conversation, speaking now of the Pickerings, and now of some common friends in London; the people, in fact, who had brought these two together.

"They knew I had come out here; didn't they tell you?"

"I never went near them again."

This answer set Ferrers thinking; and, after refilling the girl's pannikin and cutting more damper, he took a saddle from a long peg. He must catch his horse, he said; he would come back and see how she was getting on.

He did not come back for nearly an hour: the horse was a young one, and the horse-paddock, which was some little distance beyond the hut, was absurdly large. He returned ultimately at a gallop, springing off, with a new eagerness in his face, at the door of the hut. It was empty. He searched the hut, but the girl was gone. Then he remounted, and rode headlong down the fence; and something that he saw soon enough made his spurs draw blood. She was lying in the full glare of the morning sun, sound asleep. He had difficulty in awakening her, and greater difficulty in dissuading her from lying down again where she was.

"Have you spent half a summer up here without learning to respect the back-block sun? You mustn't think of going to sleep in it again. It's as much as your life is worth."

"Which is very little," murmured Miss Winfrey, letting some sand slip through her fingers, as if symbolically.

"Look here!" said Ferrers. "I shall be out all day, seeing to the sheep and riding the boundaries. There's a room at the back of my hut which the boss and those young fellows use whenever they stay there. They keep some blankets in it, but I have the key. The coach doesn't go till eight o'clock to-night. Why not lie down there till five or six?"

"I'm not a fool in everything," said the girl at length. "I'll do that."

"Then jump on my horse."

"That I can't do!"

"I'll give you a hand."

"I should fall off!"

"Not at a walk. Besides, I'll lead him. Recollect you've nine miles before you this evening."

She gave in. The room proved comfortable. She fell asleep to the sound of the horse's canter, lost in a few strides in the sand, but continuous in her brain. And this time she slept for many hours.

It was a heavy, dreamless sleep, from which she at last awoke refreshed, but entirely nonplussed as to her whereabouts. The room was very small and hot. It was also remarkably silent, but for the occasional crackling of the galvanised roof; and rather dark, but for the holes which riddled that roof like stars, letting in so many sunbeams as thin as canes. Miss Winfrey held her watch in one of them, but it had stopped for want of winding. Then she opened the door, and the blazing sun was no higher in the west than it had been in the east when last she saw it.

On a narrow bench outside her door stood a tin basin, with a bit of soap in it, cut fresh from the bar; a coarse but clean towel; and a bucket of water underneath. The girl crept back into the room, and knelt in prayer before using these things. In the forenoon none of them had been there.

Going round presently to the front of the hut, the first thing she saw was the stockrider's boots, with the spurs on them, standing just outside the door; within there was a merry glare, and Wilfrid Ferrers cooking more chops in his stocking soles before a splendid fire.

"Well!" she exclaimed in the doorway, for she could not help it.

"Awake at last!" he cried, turning a face ruddy from the fire. "You've had your eight hours. It's nearly five o'clock."

"Then I must start instantly."

"Time enough when we've had something to eat."

The first person plural disconcerted her. Was he coming too? Mr. Pickering had taken it for granted that they would go together; he was sending another man to look after the out-station; but then Mr. Pickering was labouring under a delusion; he did not understand. Wilfrid was very kind, considering that his love for her was dead and buried in the dead past. The gentleman was not dead in him, at all events. How cleverly he managed those hissing chops! He looked younger in the firelight, years younger than in the cold grey dawn. But no wonder his love of her was dead and gone.

"Now we're ready," he cried at last. "Quick, while they're hot, Lena!" His tone had changed entirely since the early morning; it was brisker now, but markedly civil and considerate. He proceeded to apologise for making use of her Christian name; it had slipped out, he said, without his thinking.

At this fresh evidence of his indifference, the girl forced a smile, and declared it did not matter.

"Surely we can still be friends," said she.

"Yes, friends in adversity!" he laughed. "Don't you feel as if we'd been wrecked together on a desert island? I do. But what do you think of the chops?"

"Very good for a desert island."

She was trying to adopt his tone; it was actually gay; and herein his degeneracy was more apparent to her than in anything that had gone before. He could not put himself in her place; the cruel dilemma that she was in, for his sake, seemed nothing to him; his solitary dog's life had deprived him of the power of feeling for another. And yet the thought of those boots outside in the sand contradicted this reflection; for he had put them on soon after her reappearance, thus showing her on whose account they had been taken off. Moreover, his next remark was entirely sympathetic.

"It's very rough on you," he said. "What do you mean to do?"

"I suppose I must go back to Melbourne."

"And then?"

"Get another place—if I can."

He said no more; but he waited upon her with heightened assiduity during the remainder of their simple meal; and when they set out together—he with all his worldly goods in a roll of blankets across his shoulders—she made another effort to strike his own note of kindly interest and impersonal sympathy. "And you," she said as they walked; "what will *you* do?"

"Get a job at the next station; there'll be no difficulty about that."

"I'm thankful to hear it."

"But I *am* in a difficulty about you."

He paused so long that her heart fluttered, and she knew not what was coming. They passed the place where her resolution had given way in the dark hour before the dawn; she recognised that other spot, where, later, he had found her asleep in the sun; but the first fence was in sight before he spoke.

"I can't stand the idea of your putting in another appearance in the township," he exclaimed at last, thrilling her with the words, which expressed perhaps the greatest of her own immediate dreads. "It won't do at all. Things will have got about. You must avoid the township at all costs."

"How can I?"

"By striking the road much lower down. It will mean bearing to the right, and no more beaten tracks after we get through this gate. But the distance will be the same and I know the way."

"But my trunks——"

"The boss said he would have them put on the coach. They'll probably be aboard whether you are or no. If they aren't, I'll have them sent after you."

"I shall be taking you out of your way," objected the girl.

"Never mind. Will you trust me?"

"Most gratefully."

She had need to be grateful. Yes, he was very kind; he was breaking her heart with his kindness, that heart which she had read backward five years ago, but aright ever since. It was all his. Either the sentiment which was one of her inherent qualities, or the generosity which was another, or both, had built up a passion for the man she had jilted, far stronger than any feeling she could have entertained for him in the early days of their love. She had yearned to make atonement, and having prayed, for years, only to meet him again, to that end, she had regarded her prayer now as answered. But answered how cruelly! Quite an age ago, he must have ceased to care; what was worse, he had no longer any strong feelings about her, one way or the other. Oh, that was the worst of all! Better his first hot scorn, his momentary brutality: she had made him feel then: he felt nothing now. And here they were trudging side by side, as silent as the grave that held their withered love.

They came to the road but a few minutes before the coach was due. Ferrers carried no watch; but he had timed their journey accurately by the sun. It was now not a handbreadth above the dun horizon; the wind had changed, and was blowing fresh from the south; and it was grateful to sit in the elongated shadows of two blue-bushes which commanded a fair view of the road. They had been on the tramp upwards of two hours; during the second hour they had never spoken but once, when he handed her his water-bag; and now he handed it again.

"Thank you," she said, passing it back after her draught. "You have been very kind!"

"Ah, Lena!" he cried, without a moment's warning, "had you been a kinder girl, or I a stronger man, we should have been happy enough first or last! Now it's too late. I have sunk too low. I'd rather sink lower still than trade upon your pity."

"Is that all?"

"That's all."

He pointed to a whirl of sand half a mile up the road. It grew larger, giving glimpses of half-harnessed horse-flesh and heavily revolving wheels. The girl's lips moved; she could hear the driver's whip, cracking louder and louder; but the words came hard.

"It is not true," she cried at last. "That is not all. You—don't—care!"

He turned upon her his old, hungry eyes, so sunken now. "I do," he said hoarsely. "Too much—to drag you down. No! let me sink alone. I shall soon touch bottom!"

She got to her feet. The coach was very near them now, the off-lamp showing up the vermilion panels; the bits tinkling between the leaders' teeth; the body of the vehicle swinging and swaying on its leather springs. The governess got to her feet, and pointed to the coach with a helpless gesture.

"And I?" she asked him. "What's to become of me?"

The south wind was freshening with the fall of night; at that very moment it blew off the driver's wide-awake, and the coach was delayed three minutes.

A few yards farther it was stopped again, and at this second exasperation the driver's language went from bad to worse; for the coach was behind its time.

"What now? Passengers?"

"Yes."

"The owner of the boxes?"

"Yes."

"And you too? Where's your cheque?"

There was a moment's colloquy between the two dusky figures in the road; then the man took a slip of paper from the left-hand pocket in his moleskins, and held it to the off-lamp for the driver's inspection. "The two of us," he said.

"Yes? Well! up you jump.... All aboard!"

And with his blankets round her, and her hand in his, the little governess, and her lost love who was found, passed at star-rise through the Greenbush boundary-gate, and on and on into another life.

A FAREWELL PERFORMANCE

Sam Eccles had killed a brown snake in his wood-heap, and had proceeded to play a prehistoric trick on all comers to the Murrumbidgee Bridge Hotel. He had curled up the carcase under a bench on the verandah, and the new chum from Paka, riding in for the station mail, had very violently killed that snake again. But the new chum was becoming acclimatised to bush humour; and *he* arranged the lifeless coil in a most lifelike manner on the snoring body of a Gol-gol boundary-rider who was lying deathly drunk inside the bar. This a small but typical company applauded greatly; but Sam Eccles himself leant back against the wall and laughed only softly in his beard. There was a reminiscent twinkle in his eye, and someone offered him something for his thoughts.

"I was thinkin'," said Sam, "of another old snake-yarn that come my way last Christmas-time. Was any of you jokers in the township then? I thought not; it was the slackest Christmas ever I struck."

"My troubles about Christmas!" said a drover with a blue fly-veil. "Pitch us the yarn."

"Ah, but it's a yarn and a half! I'm not sure that I want to pitch it. I do and I don't; it'd make you smile."

"Yes?"

"Rip it out, Sam!"

"See here, boss," said the drover, "mix yer own pison and chalk it to me." And that settled the matter.

"Any of you know the I-talian?" began Sam, by way of preface, as he mixed his grog.

"Pasquale?" said the new chum. "Rather! I sling him out of my store periodically."

"He's our local thief," Sam explained, for the benefit of the drover and his mates, who were strangers to the township. "A real bad egg, so bad that we're proud of him. Shakes everything he can lay his dirty nails on, and smokes a meerschum he must have shook before we knew him. An organ-grinder in redooced circumstances, that's what's the matter with old Squally; but he must have been out a good bit, for he speaks as good bloomin' English as you or me. Came this way first a year or two ago; hadn't been here a month before every decent door in the place was slammed in the beggar's face. I've fired him out of this again and again. The last time was last Christmas Day. He had the cheek to shove in his ugly mug, first thing in the morning, and ask if there was any free drinks going. Free drinks for him! He went out quicker than he come in. But he turns up again in the afternoon, as bold as blessed brass, and, by cripes, I didn't fire him then!

"The joker was bit by a snake. His face was as white as his teeth, an' there was the fear o' death, yes, an' the heat of hell in his wicked eyes. He'd chucked his hat away, after ripping out the greasy blue linin', and that's what he'd got twisted around his right wrist. Twisted so tight, with the stem of his pipe, that the hand looked dead and rotten, all but a crust of blood between the knuckles. Then he licks off the blood, and there sure enough were two little holes, just like stabs, five-eighths of an inch apart. My blessed oath!

"'What kind?' says I, though I thought I knew.

"'A coral,' says Squally, as I expected. And you know what *that* means, you mister; there's not one in ten as gets bit by a coral-snake and lives to show the place."

The new chum nodded.

"Well, there was just one chance for the joker and that was all. I filled a tumbler with whisky straight—hanged if he'd touch it! Never see such a thing in my life! That swine who'd get dead drunk every time he got the slant—who'd been round that very mornin', cadgin' for a drink—the same obstinate pig wouldn't touch a drop now to save his life. 'No, no,' says Squally, 'I have been drunken dev-ill all my days, let me die sober, let me die sober.' So we had to take him and force that whisky down his throat, like giving a horse a ball, and another big nobbler on top of it to make sure. Then we stood round and looked on. D'ye see, mister, if it made him tight we'd pull him through; if it didn't, there was no hope for him; and there'd be one blackguard less in Riverina. Well, for a bit he stood as straight an' as firm as them verandah posts; but it wasn't long before I see his knees givin' an' his chin comin' down upon his chest; an' then I knew as all was right. In less than five minutes he was blind and speechless; we'd got him spread out comfy in that corner; and the rest of us were quenching the little thirst we'd raised over the business."

Here Sam Eccles suited the action to the word, and the drover with the blue fly-veil shook his head.

"You didn't deserve them drinks," said he. "What did you want to go and save a thing like that for? You should have let the joker die. *I* would."

"I wished I had," replied Sam, ruefully. "That's not the end of the yarn, d'ye see, and it's the end what's going to make you chaps smile. There's a rabbit inspector lives in this here township, and knows more about nat'ral history than any other two men in the back-blocks. He happened to be at home that day, and he's at home to-day, too, if you'd like to see the snake what bit the Italian. He has it in his house—and this is how he come to get it. Somebody tells him what's happened, and he looks in during the evening to see for himself. There was old Squally drowned in whisky, sleepin' like a kid. 'So,' says Mr. Gray—that's the rabbit-inspector—'now's my time. The other day I lost my pen-knife; must have dropped it out of the buggy, but remembered the place and drove back; met Squally on the way, and nat-rally never saw my knife again. Now's my time,' says he, 'to get it back. Now's the time,' he says, 'for all of us to get back everything we ever lost!' And down he goes on his knees beside Squally, and starts feeling in his pockets.

"'Here it is!' he says directly; and yet he never gets up from his knees.

"'Struck anything else, Mr. Gray?' says I at last.

"'Yes, Sam, I have,' says he, turning round and fixing me with his blue goggles. 'What sort of a snake was it our friend here said had bitten him?'

"'A coral,' says I.

"'Not it,' says he.

"'What then?' says I.

"'A new variety altogether,' says Mr. Gray, grinning through his beard.

"'Give it a name, sir,' says I.

"'Certainly,' says he, getting up. 'If we call it the knife-snake we shan't be far out.' And blowed if he didn't show me the little blade of his own knife blooded at the point; blowed if he didn't fit the blessed point into Squally's blessed bites!"

Sam covered his face for shame, but joined next moment in the laugh against himself. Not so he of the blue fly-veil. The drover's hairy visage was a strong study in perfectly candid contempt.

"You run a bush pub, and you were had by that old dodge. It hasn't got a tooth in its head—it's as old as the blooming sandhills—yet you were had. My stars!"

The new chum from Paka diverted the laugh by innocently inquiring what that dodge might be.

"A free drunk," said the drover. "And you ought to stand *us* free drinks, mister, for not knowing. You're only a shade better than our friend the boss. To swallow that old chestnut at this time o' day!"

Sam Eccles lost his temper.

"You've said about enough. The man I mean was a born actor. Either shut your blessed head or take off that coat and come outside."

"Right," replied the drover, divesting himself on his way to the door. Sam followed him with equal alacrity, but came to a sudden halt upon the threshold.

"Wait a bit!" he cried. "Jiggered if here ain't the very man I've been telling you about; running on one leg too, as if he was up to the same old dodge again. He *can't* be. It's too steep!"

Even as he spoke there was the bound of a bare foot in the verandah, and a hulking Neapolitan hopped into the bar with his other foot in his hand and apparent terror in his eyes. But his face was not white at all; it was flushed with running; and the actor seemed dazed, or disconcerted by the presence of an unknown audience.

"Bitten again?" inquired Sam Eccles, genially.

"Bitten by a coral. Bitten in my foot! Look, look at the marks. Per Dio! I am dead man. A drink—a drink!"

"Hark at that!" said Sam Eccles, nudging the man whom he had been about to fight. "You're in luck; I never thought, when I was pitching you that yarn, that you'd see the same thing over again with your own eyes. Who'd have believed he'd try the same game twice? But don't he do it well?" And as Sam said this, he wrested the whisky-bottle from Pasquale's hands, and put that worthy down on his back.

"No, you don't. Not this time, Squally. Not much!"

The Neapolitan was up again in an instant, foaming at the mouth, and cursing volubly, but ready hands held him back.

"You ought to have been an actor, old man," said one.

"He ought so," laughed the drover. "He's a treat. I wouldn't have missed him for a lot."

Pasquale spat in his face.

"No, no, you don't see him at his best," said Sam Eccles, apologetically. "He's over-doing it. He was three times as good last trip."

The actor turned and reviled him, struggling with his captors, kicking them harmlessly with his bare feet—gesticulating—pointing to the twin blood-spots on his left instep—and weeping prayers and curses in the same breath. But if none had heeded him at first, much less would they do so now; for he had fallen incontinently upon his native tongue.

"A damned good performance," said the drover, wiping his face. "But I guess I'll burst him when he's finished."

"I wouldn't," said the tolerant Eccles. "I let him off light last time. It's something to have an actor like him in the back-blocks. Look at that!"

The Neapolitan lay bunched and knotted on the ground in a singularly convincing collapse.

"I don't believe it's acting at all!" cried the youth from Paka, in a whinny of high excitement.

"You're a new chum," retorted Sam Eccles. "What do you know about it? You wasn't even here last time."

"I know a sham when I see one. There's not much sham about this!"

And without more words the new chum fled the bar, a shout of laughter following him out into the heat.

"These young chaps from home, they know so much," said Sam Eccles. "I tell you what, our friend was drunk this trip before he come in. That's what made him pile it on so. He's as paralytic now as he was last time after them two tumblers of whisky. Let's stick him in the same old corner, and drink his bloomin' health."

The company did so while Sam refilled the glasses.

"Here's to old Squally the I-talian. Otherwise Lion Comique of the Riverina district of Noo South Wales. Long life an' 'ealth to 'em—hip, hip, hurray!"

Sam made the speech and led the cheers. His late antagonist and he clinked glasses and shook hands; then Sam pointed to the heap of moleskin and Crimean shirting, in the far corner of the bar, and lowered his voice.

"You've not seen him at his best," he insisted. "The beggar was too blooming drunk to start with."

"I'll see him when he's sober," said the drover grimly. "But he can act!"

"My oath! Sober *or* drunk. Hullo, here *is* a joke; blowed if that new chum hasn't fetched Mr. Gray to have a look at old Squally, just like he did before!"

And the two men paused to watch the rabbit-inspector, who had entered without looking their way, kneel down beside the prostrate Pasquale, and bend over him with blue spectacles intent. He examined the punctures on the left instep; he stooped and sucked them with his lips. His next act was to raise one eyelid after another; his last, to lay a weather-beaten hand upon the Italian's heart; and all this was done in a dead silence which had fallen upon the place with the entry of Mr. Gray.

"Long life to 'im again," murmured the drover, emptying his glass; but Sam Eccles neither heard nor answered him. At length the inspector arose, and turned towards them with his expressionless glasses.

"There was no nonsense about it this time, Sam. It was a snake right enough, and a coral-snake into the bargain."

Sam gave a gasping cry.

"But if he's drunk——"

"He isn't; he's dead."

In his own corner the Gol-gol boundary-rider lay snoring through it all, a dead snake still curled upon his breast.

A SPIN OF THE COIN

Unfortunately the young man was not by any means the genius he looked, with his pale, keen face and hungry eyes: or fortunately, as some may say: since there is now no occasion to grieve for him on national grounds. For the rest, he had none so near to him as to provoke your sympathy with the living, being either unable or else unwilling to claim any sort of kinship with others of his name. In fine he was without a friend in the world, save one only, who swore to wait for him, if need be, till she became an old, old woman.

We will call him Saumerez, and his friend Sapphira.

They had met in a crowded studio where women of all ages, and a few young men, may either work or play at drawing the figure, under the tutelage of one of the clever failures of his profession. The girl had come to play, having tired suddenly of life in the country, and felt the aching need of a new sensation; the man to work his hardest, in the intervals of other work which by itself was quite hard enough for any one man not accurst with a soul above black-and-white work for a minor illustrated paper. But though the aims of these two were as the poles asunder, the time of their coming coincided; and the very first day, their eyes joined through the rustling, tittering forest of easels; his being black as night, and hers so soft, that it was not till he came to paint them that he gave a thought to their colour.

Sapphira had also brought with her from the country such a complexion as one might look for, but would seldom see; and it bloomed in the London studio like a fresh rose in a faded wreath. Nor was it only her good looks that fascinated the most truly artistic eye of all those around her; she was at least as remarkable, in that place, for the self-possession and good-breeding which enabled her to take her own time in making the acquaintance of her fellow-students, without seeming either lonely or self-conscious, nor yet particularly proud, meanwhile. As she afterwards confessed, however, Saumerez could not have been more interested in her—nor earlier—than she in Saumerez, who had always his own air of distinction, which, if it misled, was at any rate wholly unintentional in a young fellow wearing his dark hair as short as another's, and his pale face as scrupulously shaven. And, for that matter, Saumerez was easily the best workman in the studio, having talent and a professional touch, with hitherto a clean heart for his work, and a pure yearning to do more than it was in him ever to do, soon to be exchanged for the godless ambition to make money and a name.

The change, however, was quite gradual. In a mixed school of art the more austere conventions are out of place; even Sapphira learned to lay them aside with her gloves and umbrella during working hours; but she took care to make neither herself nor her friend conspicuous, as seemed to be studio fashion. Nor is it absolutely necessary to confine to the academic precincts any friendship struck up within them. Yet though it was at the first blush of the New Year that Sapphira had come up to town with an old governess (now her timid slave), springtime was well advanced before Saumerez was admitted to her little flat in Kensington. And it was only in April that his own ill-favoured studio in a grimy street off Fitzroy Square, became the scene of some sittings which produced the one good thing he ever did; and in the fatal month following that he and Sapphira spent a long delirious day in Richmond Park, and from the deer and bracken and the greening trees, came back to town engaged.

At her wish, laughingly assented to by one who for his part had nobody to tell, the engagement was kept secret for the time being. Special care was taken that it should not be guessed at the school, where engagements were painfully common, and of a brazen character invariably. On the other hand, Sapphira's duenna (and she alone) was told outright, being tame enough to trust, and for reasons of obvious expediency besides. Her sleep it spoilt for many a summer's night; and a frightened, sorrowful look which would shadow her plain old face under the young man's eyes, now aglow with a fearful fervour, worried him also in the end; until, little as it mattered to him personally, the clandestine element began to interfere with his happiness by galling his self-respect.

So one day as they sat together in Kensington Gardens, which were conveniently close to the flat, and talked over her approaching holiday (Sapphira was going home for August at least), Saumerez said impulsively, though with the exceeding tenderness which he could not separate from his lightest word to his mistress:

"Dearest heart, if only your people knew!"

"If only your picture were painted!" answered Sapphira. After which you can hardly need telling that he had already conceived a masterpiece, and talked it over with Sapphira, who had latterly become hotly impatient for its production.

"Ah," he said, "don't hurry me over that! I didn't intend to touch it for years and years. Heaven knows I mean no reproach to you, dearest; yet if it wasn't for my love I wouldn't think of it even now. Oh, don't look like that! I am grateful to you—I am, indeed, for hurrying me up; I was just as likely to go to the other extreme. But you must give me till next spring, sweetheart, and then——"

His eyes strayed far away into the cool, dark shadows beneath the trees, but in a flash came back to burn themselves into hers.

"My picture's painted already," he said with a smile and a meaning stare of love and worship—"the best I shall ever do. I could never love anything I did as I love my poor libel on you! Oh, but if you knew how you watch over me all the time I am at work! If you knew how one good look at you gives me fresh heart, fresh hope, fresh energy when my own stock runs out! For it is you sometimes, though I made it. And yet, now I am with you, I see it is no more you than a smear of blue paint is the sky—my darling heart!"

His passion pleased Sapphira, and put out of her head for the moment the thought of her people, which haunted her unpleasantly at times; but as decidedly such a time was the present, when she was about to go back into their midst, she reverted to the subject of her own accord, dwelling chiefly on the obsolete character of her people's ideas on certain points, of which the instance was the fuss they had made about her coming up to town at all. That move had obtained their sanction at last, but never their approval. They were still on the pounce for the slightest pretext to insist upon her giving it all up, like a dutiful child, which (said Sapphira) was by no means their opinion of her in the meantime. If, therefore, they were to suspect for one moment—but imperatively they must suspect nothing until such time as they might be told all with confidence born of a picture in the Academy at the very least. Such were the girl's people on her own showing. As a fact, they were also exceedingly prosperous and well-to-do; but of that she made as little as possible. And a few days later she was back among them; taking nothing seriously from morning till night; joining heartily in the general laugh against herself and her artistic exploits in town; and cheerfully supporting, from day to day, the renewed attentions of a young neighbouring squire, whom she had banished from the country (without intending that) a twelve-month before—the honest gentleman, in fact, who is now her husband.

Meanwhile in glaring London, the ill-starred Saumerez was wearing out brain and hand and eye for his Sapphira. As a moving surprise for her when she returned, and to show his great love, he had begun incontinently upon his great attempt; and daily the dream of months was crumbling beneath his hand, for the simple reason that the conception was entirely beyond his present power of execution, besides being as yet most imperfectly matured in his mind. Hour after hour, and day after day, his hand hovered over the great canvas, as often with palette-knife as with brush; and only the presence of his model kept him from tears and execrations. And night after night, under a great blinding light, the same fool sat drawing viciously for the semi-insolvent illustrated paper from which he was earning his precarious livelihood all this time. Night and day, day and night; it was enough to wreck the strongest, and Saumerez was never strong. But he was greatly fortified by the thought of his mistress, and still more by the ever-present sight of her on the one canvas he had covered to something like his own satisfaction. Sapphira's portrait was a distinct success, which left him some lingering belief in his own powers, to pit against daily and hourly failure; and he had often told her how it encouraged him in another way. By a clever trick accidently caught he had painted her eyes so that they watched him incessantly, whether at night over his drawing-board or at his easel during the day; he had only to look up to meet the soft eyes he loved; and sometimes, when long hours had tangled his nerves, to surprise a kind smile on the red lips and to fancy the sweet sunburnt throat swelling with warm breath. At such moments he would go and stand, until he ached again, before the portrait that was making him work desperately but not well—and think—and think—and even pray to Sapphira for pluck and power, as to a painted Virgin.

But he had made to himself a kinder face than he was ever to see any more in the flesh. For when Sapphira came back in September it was to get rid of her flat at the end of the quarter; and when he went to say good-bye to her she informed him—with considerable agitation, it is true, but yet with a firmness and decision about which there could be no mistake—that she must give him up too. In the condition to which Saumerez had reduced himself by overwork and worry, a scene was to be expected, and he made one that frightened dreadfully the author of all this misery; yet she bore it with such a disarming humility and so many and bitter self-reproaches that the wronged man's heart softened hopelessly before he left her. Thus they parted with tears on both sides, and on his the most passionate vows he had ever made her: just because she had told him how she honoured and admired him above all men, among whom, simply, she found there was none she could "really love."

Now mark the mischief of this assurance. To Saumerez it was food and drink and sleep for many days. From an only consolation it grew into a last hope. Then the hope began to importune for expression, and that crescendo, until Saumerez sat down at last and made a full and final outpouring of his soul to Sapphira, and charging her not to answer until her heart was changed, turned to his tools with relief, and began excellently by destroying the abortive "masterpiece." However, an answer came with startling promptitude. And Saumerez would have done well to open it without first pondering the superscription in the dear familiar hand, that danced through his starting tears, and without wasting time in fond and fatuous speculations; for the answer was, what Sapphira had hoped to spare him "for a long, long time"—namely, that she was already engaged to someone else—meaning the excellent man she married before the year was out.

But it was still early in October when the affair took its final turn, so far as Saumerez was concerned. In the raw afternoon of that same day he was seen in Piccadilly, walking west. His dark eyes were sunken and lack-lustre; an inky stubble covered the lower part of his face without hiding the hollows of his cheeks; and he was for passing a moderately close acquaintance with no more than a nod, but this the other would not allow.

"I say, Saumerez," cried he, "in God's name, what have you been doing?"

"Working," Saumerez answered mechanically. "I have been working rather hard. Rather too hard. I don't think I have been asleep this year. Now I am trying a little exercise."

The man he had met recommended him to try more particular remedies than that, and named a specialist for insomnia. But he found himself giving advice to strangers; for yards of greasy pavement, with its shifting freight of damp humanity, already separated him from Saumerez, whom he watched out of sight with a shrug, and put out of mind in five minutes.

In Kensington Gardens a ground fog clung to the dingy grass, shrouding the trunks of trees whose tops were sharp enough against a merely colourless sky. It was the first afternoon that autumn when your breath smoked in the air. The use of the place on such a day was as a route, not a retreat, and Saumerez had no fellow loiterers. But ever through the fog the leaves floated softly to the ground—a meagre, unnoticeable shower, of no conceivable interest to anybody; yet Saumerez watched it attentively till the light failed, sitting the whole time on a seat that would have chilled to the bone any person in his proper senses. It was a seat, however, on which he remembered sitting with Sapphira once in the summer before she went away. He sat on now until a keeper in a cape stopped to tell him it was half-past five and he must go. He got up at once, and walked home; but God knows by what roundabout way; for when he reached his studio the moon was teeming into it through the top-light, and shining with all its weight on Sapphira as Saumerez had painted her.

The eyes were on him from the moment he crossed the threshold; and still they seemed to smile; but he shut the door, and went up close, as he had gone a hundred times before, and gave them back a ghastly grin.

"You devil!" he said quietly. "You little, lying devil!" And he said worse, but all so quietly. And as he swore and grinned he took out his pen-knife, and without looking at it ran his thumb over the blade and threw the knife away. It was too blunt for him. So he flung through the studio, upsetting with a crash a table laden with brushes and pipes and a soup-plateful of ashes, and clattered down the step into the bedroom which adjoined. The eyes were waiting for him when he came back with a lighted candle in his left hand and in his right an open razor, which he plunged with a curse into the brown slender throat. But still the eyes met his gaily, and for that, and because the canvas would not bleed, he slit and hacked at it until the wooden frame was empty, and the moon shining through showed the painted shreds of canvas on the floor.

Then Saumerez laughed stupidly, and repeated the laugh at intervals until the moon flashed in his eyes from the open razor still between his fingers. After that he stood as still as of old when worshipping his picture. But at length he changed the razor to the hand which held the candle-stick, for a moment, while he poised a shilling on his thumb-nail.

"Heads for hell!" he called aloud. The coin spun upward into the skylight, and came spinning down through the moonbeams; it rang on the floor and rolled away.

On his knees Saumerez hunted for it, the open razor grasped once more in his right hand, the candle dripping from his left; while he repeated, as though their aptness pleased him, the words "sudden death." But the shilling was not to be discovered instantly; it had rolled among the débris of the fallen table; and when found it was so coated with tobacco-ash that which side was uppermost it was impossible to tell. Saumerez would not touch the tossed coin; but he craned his neck downward, blew away the ashes, and grinned again as he tightened his grip.

.   .   .   .

THE STAR OF THE *GRASMERE*

My acquaintance with Jim Clunie began and ended on the high seas. It began when the good ship *Grasmere*, of the well-known Mere line of Liverpool clippers, was nine days out from that port, bound for Melbourne with a hardware cargo and some sixty passengers. There were but seven of us, however, in the saloon, and Clunie was not of this number. He was a steerage passenger. When, therefore, on the tenth day out I had occasion to seek the open air in the middle of dinner, I was not a little surprised to find Clunie practically in possession of the poop. As a steerage passenger he had no business to be there at all, much less with the revolver which I instantly noticed in his right hand.

"It's all right, my lord," he shouted to me hesitating on the top of the ladder. "I'm only taking a pot at the sea-gulls." And he discharged his weapon over the rail, needless to say without effect, for we were close-hauled to a hard head wind, and pitching violently.

I looked at the man at the wheel, and the man at the wheel nodded to me.

"The third mate'll be back in a minute, sir. He's only gone for'ard to speak to Chips."

"A minute's all I want," cried Clunie, firing twice in quick succession. "What does your lordship say? Too jolly sick to say anything, eh?"

I need hardly explain that I have no title, and just then I was neither nature's nobleman nor lord of creation, as I hung and clung like a wet towel to the rail. But such manhood as I retained was still sensitive to an impertinence, and I turned and stared as resentfully as possible at this impudent fellow. He was young enough, but I was younger, and I feel sure we hated each other on the spot. At my look, at all events, his offensive grin changed to a sinister scowl, while I recollect making an envious note of his biceps, which filled out the sleeves of the striped football jersey that he wore instead of a coat. Perhaps at the same moment he was looking at my wrists, which are many sizes too small, for the next liberty the brute took was to pat me on the back with his left hand while he brandished the smoking revolver in his right.

"Cheer up," said he. "You'll be as good a man as any of us when we get the trades. Try sardines whole! When you can keep a whole sardine you'll be able to keep anything."

"The third mate'll be up directly," said the man at the wheel.

"He will so!" said I, starting off to fetch him; but as I reached the break of the poop, up came the captain himself, who had heard the shots, and in a very few seconds Mr. Clunie found himself in his proper place upon the main deck. He took his discomfiture very coolly, however, just nodding and laughing when the captain threatened to take away his revolver altogether. And I saw no more of the man for some days, because I was so cold on deck that I soon retired to the saloon settee, and so miserable on the saloon settee that I finally retreated to my own berth, where indeed most of my time was being spent.

For the voyage had begun badly enough, but for three weeks it went from bad to worse. We were actually three weeks in beating clear of the Bay of Biscay, during which time we were constantly close-hauled, but never on the same tack for more than four consecutive hours. It was a miserable state of things for those of us who were bad sailors. For four hours one's berth was at such an angle that one could hardly climb out of it; for four more the angle was reversed, and one lay in continual peril of being shot across the cabin like clay from a spade. Then the curtains, the candle-stick and one's clothes on the pegs described arcs that made one sick to look at them; and yet there was nothing else to look at except the port-hole, which was washed repeatedly by great green seas that darkened the cabin and shook the ship. The firm feet and hearty voices of the sailors overhead, when all hands put the ship about at eight bells, were only less aggravating than the sound and smell of the cuddy meals that reached and tortured me three times a day. I think my single joy during those three weeks was one particularly foul morning on the skirts of the Bay, when I heard that all the ham and eggs for the cuddy breakfast had been washed through the lee scupper-holes. Ham and eggs in a sea like that!

Most days, it is true, I did manage to crawl on deck, but I could never stand it for long. I had not found my sea-legs, my knees were weak, and I went sliding about the wet poop like butter on a hot plate. The captain's hearty humour made me sad. The patronising airs of a couple of consumptives, who were too ill to be sick, filled my heart with impotent ire. What I minded most, however, was the open insolence of Jim Clunie. He was as good a sailor as our most confirmed invalid, and was ever the first person I beheld as I emerged from below with groping steps and grasping fingers. He seemed to spend all his time on the after-hatch, always in his blue and black football jersey and a Tam o' Shanter, and generally with a melodeon and some appreciative comrade, whom he would openly nudge as I appeared. I can see him now, with his strong, unshaven, weather-reddened face, and his short, thick-set, athletic frame; and I can hear his accursed melodeon. Once he struck up "The Conquering Hero" as I laboriously climbed the starboard ladder.

Never were three longer weeks; but a fair wind came at last, and came to stay. We took the northeast trades in 29° N., and thenceforward we bowled along in splendid style, eight or nine knots an hour, with a slight permanent list to port, but practically no motion. The heavy canvas was taken down, the ship put on her summer suit of thin white sails, and every stitch bagged out with steadfast wind. There was now no need to meddle with the yards, and the crew were armed with scrapers and paint-pots to keep them out of mischief. Awnings were spread, as every day the sun grew hotter and the sea more blue, and under them the passengers shot up like flowers in a forcing-house. There was an end to our miseries, and the pendulum swung to the other extreme. I never saw so many souls in spirits so high or in health so blooming. We got to know each other; we told stories; we sang songs; we organized sweepstakes on the day's run. We played quoits and cards, draughts and chess. We ventured aloft, were duly pursued and mulcted in the usual fine. We got up a concert. We even started a weekly magazine.

And in almost everything my foe Clunie took conspicuous part. He was the only man of us who was too quick for the sailors up aloft. When his pursuer had all but reached him, Clunie swung himself on to one of the stays and slid from the cross-trees to the deck in the most daring fashion, thus exempting himself from further penalty. He afterwards visited all three mastheads in one forenoon, and wrote his name on the truck of each. We had our first concert the same evening, and if one man contributed to its success more than another, that man was undoubtedly Jim Clunie. He not only played admirably upon his melodeon, but he recited "The Charge of the Light Brigade" and Poe's "Raven" with unsuspected force and cleverness. People began to speak of him as the life and soul of the ship, and yet in the saloon we were getting to like him less and less. For though plucky and talented, he was also pushing, overbearing, and ready to make himself objectionable on or without the very slightest provocation.

He had sent in a contribution for the *Grasmere Chronicle*, which happened to be edited by the doctor and myself. We were prepared for a good thing, for the general aggressiveness of the man had by no means blinded us to his merits, but we soon discovered that these did not include any sort of literary faculty. His effusion was too silly even for a ship's magazine. It was also illiterate, so it really did fall short of our modest standard. We rejected it, and that night I encountered Clunie in the waist of the ship.

"You call yourself the editor of the *Grasmere Chronicle*, do ye not?" he began, stopping me, and speaking with the northern burr that gave some little distinction to his speech. I had noticed that this burr accentuated itself under the influence of emotion, and it was certainly accentuated now. So I looked at him inquiringly, and he rolled out his words afresh and rather louder.

"I am one of the editors," said I.

"Yes; the one that rejected my verses!" cried he, with a great many r's in the last word.

"No," I said, "I'm afraid we did that between us."

"That's a lie," said he through his teeth, "and you know it's a lie. You're the man! You're the man! And see here, my fine friend, I'll be even with 'e before we get to—the port we're bound for. D'ye know what that is?"

"Melbourne," said I.

"Kingdom Come!" said he; "and I'll pay you out before we get there."

The sun had been very hot. I felt sure that it had struck through Clunie's most unsuitable Tam o' Shanter and affected his brain. Nothing else could explain the absurd ferocity of his tone about so trivial and impersonal a matter as a rejected offering for our magazine. His face it was too dark to see, but I went straight to the doctor and reported my suspicions.

"If you don't prescribe that man a straw hat," said I, "you may order a sheet and a shot for this one; for I'll swear he means to murder me."

The doctor laughed.

"My dear fellow, it isn't that," he said. "It's much more likely to be whisky. He was as right as rain when he was with me an hour or two ago. He came to tell me what he was going to do for us to-morrow night at the concert. He means to bring the ship down this time; he's our star, my boy, and we mustn't take him too seriously; it'll never do to go and have a row with Jim Clunie."

The doctor thought differently a day or two later; meantime he took the chair at our second concert, held in 6° N., and in his opening speech he paid Clunie what I considered a rather unnecessary compliment, which, however, the "star" certainly justified before our entertainment was over. He gave us a capital selection on his melodeon, then he sang to it, concluding with a breakdown in response to a double encore. But his great success was scored in the second part of the programme, when he recited "The Dream of Eugene Aram" with a tragic intensity which has not since been surpassed in my hearing. Perhaps the tragedy was a little overdone; perhaps the reciter ranted in the stanzas descriptive of the murder; but I confess I did not think so at the time. To me there was murder in the lowered voice, and murder in the protruding chin (on which the beard was still growing), and murder in the rolling eye that gleamed into mine oftener than I liked in the course of the recitation. The latter was the most realistic performance I had ever heard, and also the most disagreeable. Nor can I have been alone in thinking so, for, when it was over, a deep sigh preceded the applause. This was deafening, but Clunie was too good an artist to risk an anti-climax by accepting his encore. He was content, possibly, to have pulled the cork out of the rest of the entertainment, which fell very flat indeed. Then, in a second speech, our infatuated doctor paid a second compliment to "the star of the *Grasmere*." And by midnight he had the star on his hands: sunstruck, it was suspected: in reality as mad as a man could be.

Some details of his madness I learned afterwards, but more I witnessed on the spot.

At six bells in the first watch he appeared half-dressed on the poop and requested the captain to make it convenient to marry him next morning. Our astonished skipper had taken his pipe from his teeth, but had not answered, when Clunie broke away with the remark that he had still to ask the girl. In a minute or two he was back, laughing bitterly, snapping his fingers, and announcing in the same breath how his heart was broken, and that he did not care. It appeared that, with a most unmerited proposal of marriage, he had been frightening the wits out of some poor girl in the steerage, whither he now returned (as he said) to sleep it down. The chief officer was sent after him, to borrow his pistols. Clunie lent them on condition the mate should shoot *me* with them, and heave my body overboard, and never let him set eyes on me again. And in the mate's wake went our dear old doctor, who treated the maniac for sun-stroke, and pronounced him a perfect cure in the morning.

Nevertheless he was seen at mid-day perched upon the extreme weather-end of the fore-t'-gallan' yard-arm, holding on to nothing, but playing his melodeon to his heart's content. The whole ship's company turned out to watch him, while the chief officer himself went aloft to coax him down. To him Clunie declared that he could see Liverpool as plain as a pike-staff on the port bow, that he could read the time by the town-hall clock, and that he wasn't coming down till he could step right off at the docks. Our ingenious chief was, however, once more equal to the occasion, and at last induced Clunie to return to the deck in order to head a mutiny and take command of the ship. When he did reach the deck, he rushed straight for me, the mate tripped him up, and in another minute he was wailing and cursing, and foaming at the mouth, with the irons on his wrists and a dozen hands holding him down. It appeared that the two of them had arranged, up aloft, to burn me alive as an offering to Neptune on crossing the line; to behead the captain and all the male passengers; and to make all females over the age of thirty walk the plank that afternoon. The last idea must have emanated from our wicked old chief himself.

They put him first in the second mate's cabin, which opened off the passage leading to the saloon. His language, however, was an unsavoury accompaniment to our meals, and it was generally felt that this arrangement could not be permanent. Though shackled hand and foot, and guarded day and night by an apprentice, he managed to escape, in a false nose and very little else, on the second afternoon. A number of us effected his capture on the main deck, but I was the only one whose action in the matter he appeared to resent. He spent the rest of that day in hoarsely cursing me from the second mate's berth. On the morrow we lost the trade-wind, which had carried us nearly to the line. All day we wallowed in a stream of rain upon an oily sea. But the damp of the doldrums seemed to suit the poor fellow in the second mate's cabin; at all events, his behaviour improved; and in a couple of days (when we were fortunate enough to drift into the south-east trades) the carpenter's berth, in the for'ard deck-house, was ready for his reception, with a sheet of iron over the door, stout bars across the port-hole, and the carpenter's locker securely screwed up.

It took Clunie exactly twenty-four hours to break into that locker. He then stationed himself at his port-hole with a small broadside of gouges and chisels, which he poised between the bars and proceeded to fire at all comers. The officers were fetched to overpower him, but Clunie managed to break the third mate's head in the fray. Then, because they could not throw him overboard, they fixed a ring-bolt in the floor of the carpenter's berth, and handcuffed Clunie down to that whenever he became violent. As we sailed into cooler latitudes, however, his mania abated day by day. He gave up railing at every man, woman, or child who passed his port-hole; he even ceased to revile me when we met on deck, where he was now allowed to take the air with his right wrist handcuffed to the left of the strongest seaman in the forecastle. And at this stage I fear that poor Clunie was the amusement of many who had latterly gone in terror of him, for he was very strong on mesmerism, which he fancied he achieved by rattling his manacles in our ears, while he was ever ready to talk the most outrageous balderdash to all who cared to listen to him. His favourite delusion was a piece of profanity, sadly common in such cases; his chief desire, to be allowed to row himself back to Liverpool in one of the boats.

"Give me the dinghy and a box of mixed biscuits," he used to say, "and that little girl who wouldn't marry me, and I won't trouble you any more."

It was all very sad, but the violent phase had been the worst. His only violence now was directed against his own outfit, which he dismembered suit after suit, swathing his feet with the rags. The striped football jersey alone survived, and this he wore in a way of his own. Because he had torn up all his trousers, he thrust his legs through the tight striped sleeves; and as his costume was completed by a strait-waistcoat, constructed by the sailmaker, it was impossible not to smile at the ludicrous figure now cut by this irresponsible soul. He was no longer dangerous. The homicidal tendency had disappeared, and with it the particular abhorrence with which I of all people had been unfortunate enough to inspire him when he was still comparatively sane. We were now quite friendly. He called me Brother John, after a character in a comic song with which I had made rather a hit at our first concert, but the familiarity was employed without offence.

We had it very cold in our easting. We all but touched the fiftieth parallel. But we were rewarded with excellent winds, and we bade fair to make a quick passage in spite of our sluggish start. One wild, wet evening, I was standing on the weather side of the quarter-deck, when Clunie came up to me with his strange apparel soaked through, his swathed feet dragging behind him like squeegees, and the salt spray glistening in his beard.

"Well, governor," said he, "do you remember refusing my verses?"

"I do," said I, smiling.

"So do I," said he, thrusting his face close to mine. "So do I, Brother John!" And he turned on his swaddled heel without another word.

Straight I went to the doctor.

"Doctor," said I, "you oughtn't to let that fellow go loose. I fear him, doctor; I fear him—horribly."

"Why?" cried he. "You don't mean to tell me he's getting worse again?"

"No," I said, "he's getting better every day; and that's exactly where my fear comes in."

The wind blew strong and fair until we were within a day's sail of Port Phillip Heads. Then it veered, still blowing strong, and we were close-hauled once more, the first time for eight weeks. Then it shifted right round, and finally it fell. So we rolled all night on a peaceful, starlit sea, with the wind dead aft and the mizzen-mast doing all the work, but that was very little. Three knots an hour was the outside reckoning, and our captain was an altered man. But we passengers gave a farewell concert, and spent the night in making up the various little differences of the voyage, and not one of us turned in till morning. Even then I for one could not sleep. I was on the brink of a new life. The thought filled me with joy and fear. We had seen no land for eighty days. We expected to sight the coast at daybreak. I desired to miss none of it. I wanted to think. I wanted air. I wanted to realise the situation. So I flung back my blankets at two bells, and I slipped into my flannels. In another minute I was running up the foremast ratlines, with a pillar of idle canvas, and a sheaf of sharp, black cordage a-swing and a-sway between me and the Australian stars.

I had not "paid my footing" at the beginning of the voyage for nothing. I had acquired a sure foot aloft, a ready hand, and, above all, a steady head. I climbed to the cross-trees without halt or pause, and then I must needs go higher. My idea was to sit on the royal yard, and wait there for Australia and the rising sun. It is the best spar for seeing from, because there are no sails to get in your way—you are on the top of all. But it is also the slightest, the least stable, and the farthest from the deck.

I sat close to the mast, with my arm (so to speak) round its waist; and it is extraordinary how much one sees from the fore-royal yard. There was no moon that night, the sea seemed as vast as the sky and almost as concave. Indeed, they were as two skies, joined like the hollows of two hands: the one spattered with a million moonstones; the other all smeared with phosphorous; both inky, both infinite; and, perched between the two, an eighteen-year-old atom, with fluttering heart and with straining eyes, on the edge of a wide new world.

It had been a pleasant voyage. I was sorry it was over. Captain, officers, passengers and crew, it was probably my last night among them, and my heart turned heavy at the thought. They had been good friends to me. Should I make as good over yonder? It was too much to expect; these dear fellows had been so kind. Among them all I had made but one enemy, and he, poor devil, was not accountable. My thoughts stayed a little with Clunie, who had not spoken to me since the wet wild night when he brought up that silly forgotten matter of his rejected contribution. My thoughts had not left him when his very voice hailed me from a few feet below.

"Sit tight, Brother John," he cried, softly. "I'll be with ye in two twos."

I nearly fell from the yard. He was within reach of my hand. His melodeon was slung across his shoulders, and he had a gleaming something between his teeth. It looked like a steel moustache. There would have been time to snatch it from him, to use it if necessary in my own defence. As I thought of it, however, his feet were on the foot-rope, and he himself had plucked the knife from his mouth. It was a carving-knife, and I could see that his mouth was bleeding.

"Move on a bit," he said; and when I hesitated he pricked me in the thigh. Next moment he was between the mast and me.

He thrust his left arm through my right; his own right was round the mast, and the knife was in his right hand, which he could hardly have used in that position. For an instant my heart beat high; then I remembered having seen him throw quoits with his left hand. And I heard the look-out man give a cough deep down below.

"Ay, we hear him," observed Clunie, "but he won't hear us unless you sing out. And when you do that you're a gone coon. Fine night, is it not? If we sit here long enough we shall see Australia before morning. So that surprises you, Brother John? Thought I'd say Liverpool, now, didn't you? Not me, you fool, not me. I'm as sane as you are to-night."

He chuckled, and I felt my forehead; it was cold and messy. But say something I must, so I laughed out:

"Were you ever anything else?"

"Ever anything else? I was as mad as mad, and you know it, too. You're trying to humour me; but I know that game too well, so look out!"

"You mistake me, Clunie, you do——"

"You fool!" said he; "take that, and get out further along the yard."

And he gave my leg another little stab, that brought the blood through my flannels like spilled ink. I obeyed him in order to put myself beyond his reach. This, however, was not his meaning at all. He edged after me as coolly as though we were dangling our legs over the side of a berth.

"I've got a crow to pluck with you," he went on, "and you know well enough what it is."

"Those verses?" said I, holding on with all ten fingers; for we were rolling as much as ever; and now the black sea rose under us on one side, and now on the other; but Clunie had straddled the spar, and he rode it like a rocking-horse, without holding on at all.

"Those verses," he repeated. "At least, that's one of them. I should have said there was a brace of crows."

"Well, as to the verses," said I, "you were hardly a loser. Our magazine, as you may know, died a natural death the very next week."

"Of course it did," said Clunie, with an air of satisfaction which I found encouraging. "You refused my poem, so, of course, the thing fizzled out. What else could you expect? But I tell you I have a second bone to pick with you. And you'll find it the worst of the two—for you!"

"I wonder what that is," said I, in a mystified tone, thinking to humour him still more.

"I'll tell you," said he. "Just shunt a bit further along the yard."

"I shall be over in a minute," I cried, as he forced me and followed me with the naked carver.

"I know you will," he replied, "but not till I've done with you. To come to that second bone. You had a concert to-night, and you didn't ask me to do anything!"

My teeth chattered. We had never thought of him. I protested, and truly, that the fault was not mine alone; but he cut me short.

"How many concerts have you had without asking me to perform—me, the only man of you worth listening to—me, the star o' the ship? Tell me that, Brother John!"

"I hardly know."

"Count, then!"

"I think about six."

"Curse your thinking! Make sure."

I counted with my clutching fingers.

"Seven," I said at length.

"Are ye sure?"

"Yes, perfectly."

"Then take that—and that—and that—and that!" And he pricked me in seven places with his infernal knife, holding it to my throat between the stabs in case I should sing out.

"Now," he said, "I'm going to give you a concert all to yourself. You're going to hear the star of the *Grasmere* free of charge. But get you along to the point of the spar first; then you'll be all ready. What, you won't? Ah, I thought that'd make you!"

I had obeyed him. He had followed me. And now the knife was back in his mouth—the blood had caked upon his beard—and the melodeon was between his hands. He played me the "Dead March." I should not have known it, for I was past listening, but the horrid grin in his mad eyes showed me that he was doing something clever, and then I discovered what. I was now past everything but holding on and watching my man, which, as I have since thought, was better than looking down. He was wearing his beloved jersey, and he had it the right way on. Upon his legs were a pair of thick worsted drawers; but his feet were naked, and his head was bare. It was his head I watched. His hair had been cropped very close. And the stars swam round and round it as we rose and fell.

I heard four bells struck away aft in the abyss, heard their echo from the forecastle head. It was two o'clock in the morning. As we dipped to port, Clunie suddenly lifted his melodeon in both hands, and heaved it clean over my head.

"Hear the splash?" he hissed. "Well, there'll be a bigger one in a minute, and you'll hear that. You're going to make it, Brother John!"

His words fell harmlessly on my ears. I had heard no splash. It was as though we were poised above a bottomless abyss.

The next thing I noted was the monotonous and altered sound in his voice. He was reciting "The Dream of Eugene Aram," and making the ghastliest faces close to mine as he did so. But I, too, was now astride of the spar. My legs were groping in mid-air for the brace. They found it. They clung to it. I flung myself from the spar, but the lithe, thin ropes gave with my weight, and I could not—no, I durst not let go.

And yet I was not stabbed to the heart; for there was Clunie leaning over me, with Tom Hood's stanzas still flowing from his blooded lips, and the carver held in readiness, not for me, but for the brace when I should trust myself to it. Seeing this, I held fast to the spar. But he stabbed at the back of my hand—I see the puckered white scar as I write—and I let go as we were heeling over to port. His knife flashed up among the stars. I was gone.

I wonder the rush of air in mouth and nostrils did not tear the nose from my face, the head from my body. I wonder the sea did not split me in two as I went into it like a stone. When I endeavour to recall those sensations, I invariably fail; but at times they come to me in my sleep, and when I wake the wonder is ever fresh. Yet many a man has fallen from aloft, and if he but cleared the deck, has lived to tell the tale. And I am one of that lucky number. When I came to the surface, there was the ship waggling and staggering like a wounded albatross, as they hove her to. Then they saved me in the pinnace, because I was still alive enough to keep myself afloat. But some may say that Clunie was as lucky as myself; for he had fallen a few seconds after me, and his mad brains splashed the deck.

THE END

Milton Keynes UK
Ingram Content Group UK Ltd.
UKHW010758260424
441811UK00004B/360